Where's *Mom?*

Missing Mom Finds Victory in Surrender

"Whoever loses their life for My sake, shall find it."
-Jesus Christ

By Jill Eenigenburg
with Dennis Eenigenburg

Caroline —
Joyfully His,
Jill Eenigenburg
Zeph. 3:17

ISBN: 0-9740885-0-1

First Printing July 2003

*Definitions are taken selectively out of Funk and Wagnall's Dictio-
nary. These are included in the Reflections questions at the end of
each chapter.*

Bible quotations are taken from New American Standard Bible.

Printed in the United States of America

For more information, contact:

Denjie Publishing
1227 Brutus Drive
Baton Rouge, LA 70816

eeniburg@aol.com

"The Rose"

To Jill . . .

The rose you chose,
The rose you are.
The rose was doomed,
But yet it bloomed.

The God of the rose,
To live, to blossom.
You're the one He chose,
For this we thank Him.

-From Dennis

Acknowledgments

Much love and prayer and time commitment has stimulated the compiling of this book. With heartfelt appreciation, we thank Fred and Anne Sewell, Shelley Sims, Cynthia Eenigenburg, Luanne Cotten and Sherlene Carruth. Great appreciation, too, is given for the help of Lori Ray. God has teamed all of you with us at His appointed times. God's blessings, we pray, will saturate your lives. Thank you.

Dedicated to
our sons
in the journey

and

our precious grandchildren
who will keep the
journey going ...

Table of Contents

CHAPTER ONE

Where's Mom?

by Dennis

"Hello, Dad?" It was the voice of my oldest son, Tod.

"Yes?"

"What's up?"

"Dad, Mom is not home."

I glanced at my watch. It was almost six p.m. She was always home when the boys returned from school at 4:30. A dark thought ran through my mind. Kidnapped! Recently an American General, Dozier, had been kidnapped by the Brigate Rossi in Northern Italy. As American missionaries in Rome, we were easy prey to terrorists. I regretted that my Honda Civic still carried Texas license plates.

Hiding my concern, I told Tod I would make a few phone calls. As I hung up, I recalled that Jill had a doctor's appointment around noon that day. From my office desk, I dialed the number of Dr. Stopanni, an American-trained-Italian pediatrician. Jon, our youngest son, had been suffering flu symptoms, and Jill had decided to have Dr. Stopanni examine him.

"I waited for her over an hour, but she never showed up for the appointment," Dr. Stopanni said. "I'm concerned. It's not like Jill to not call or notify us if she is not coming."

As I hung up, I looked at my watch. Over six hours had passed since the missed appointment. I called the homes of several missionary friends throughout Rome. None of them had seen or heard from Jill all day.

Anxiety mounting, I called in my secretary, Joanne Eitzen, and asked her to have one of our fellow missionaries go stay with my oldest two sons, Tod and Scot. She would also inform Paul, a co-worker, and ask him to notify the police. I would take the van and retrace the route from my apartment to the doctor's office.

As I started down Via Cimone toward Via Conca d' Oro, I wondered what I was looking for. An abandoned orange Honda Civic? A wrecked Honda Civic? My wife and son out of gas along the highway? None of these visions were comforting.

I stopped quickly at my apartment to check on the boys. I told them to pray, and that someone was coming to stay with them. At 12 and 10 years of age, they were old enough to grasp the potential seriousness of the moment.

I called my office and told Joanne I would stop at any hospital along the way just in case they had been in an accident. There were two possible routes from our apartment to the doctor's office. The longest route was up the Via Salaria, then around the ring highway called the Raccordo Annulare. I decided to check the shorter route first. The Foro Italico cut directly across the northern part of the city and would take me to the Via Cassia and Dr. Stoppani's office.

Traveling north, on the Via Cassia, I spotted a hospital. I wheeled up the driveway, found the emergency entrance, and headed toward the door at a brisk trot. By now, it was 6:45 p.m. and even in July, the shadows were lengthening.

The emergency area was alive with activity as I crossed to the desk. A woman looked up and greeted me.

"I'm looking for an American woman and a boy six years old. It's my wife and son," I said in Italian. "They have been missing all day, and I don't know if they were in an accident or what."

"Describe your wife."

"She's in her early thirties, five feet two, with blonde hair." The woman paged through her file and the seconds seemed like hours.

"I have an American boy about six years old. But I have no woman, only the boy," she replied.

"Where is he?" I asked.

"He's in that examining room across the hall."

I rushed across the hallway and gently pushed open the door, not knowing what to expect. There on the table was a boy, a blonde-haired boy. Next to him stood his mother, but he was not my son, nor was she my wife. The boy was from the nearby American community and was being treated for a cut on his hand. I apologized for interrupting and backed out of the room.

Again, I called my office. Joanne, my secretary, put Paul on the phone. Paul had news from the police. Jill and Jon had been in a car accident, but it was not serious. What a relief! They were both in a hospital called San Camillo. I thanked Paul and hung up, wondering where San Camillo was located.

"I've located my wife and son," I told the lady at the desk. "They are at San Camillo. Can you tell me how to get there?" It was obvious from her instructions that it was on the opposite side of the city. She told me which streets led in that general direction.

Entering traffic, I encountered Rome's evening rush hour. It was after seven p.m. Many Italians were heading home. Rome's four million inhabitants seemed to fill the streets with as many cars. I was in a hurry, but the buses, the cars, the trolleys all blocked my path. In addition, I didn't know where I was. Every few minutes I would stop at a flower vendor and get new directions. At 8:30 p.m., I finally arrived at San Camillo, Rome's largest hospital.

Thirty buildings were spread over four city blocks. I took the first available parking space, pushed through an opening in a fence and headed toward the closest building. Nothing but closed offices were on the first floor. Was there a nursing station upstairs? Entering the elevator, I was joined by another man—a doctor. He probably noticed my distressed look, and asked me if he could help. I related that my son and wife had been admitted after a car accident.

"What is your son's name?" he asked.

"Jon," I replied, (Giovanni, in Italian).

"I am his doctor. He is upstairs. Please wait for me there, and I will join you in a few minutes."

Later I reflected upon God's hand in my meeting this particular doctor in the midst of a 30-building complex.

The doctor exited on the third floor and I continued to the fourth floor. I didn't know what to expect.

Entering the pediatric floor, I found Jon's room and pushed open the door to see two rows of crib-like beds. The lights were already dimmed for the night. Jon spotted me, sat up, and reached his arms out toward me.

"Dad, I want to go home," he cried. "Dad, where's Mom? Is Mom home yet?"

I took him in my arms, relieved to see him conscious and not hurt, except for the largest black eye I had ever seen. It seemed to cover half his face.

Soon, the doctor arrived. He told me that Jon's condition was good, but they would like to keep him under observation. They wanted to make sure he had no internal bleeding or brain damage from the impact of the accident.

"What about my wife?" I said. A thought had been troubling me. If she was not seriously hurt, why had she not called me? I hugged Jon again and followed the doctor back to his office where he began making phone calls.

His tone of voice changed during the second call. He took notes and asked questions. I sensed that my wife's condition was indeed serious. After he hung up the phone, he looked at me and said in English, "I'm sorry. It's very bad." He explained that he was originally from Belgium and that he would give me the medical details in English. I was grateful because medical terms were not a part of my Italian vocabulary during my two and a half years in Italy.

"Your wife," he explained, "is not in this building. She is in Rianimazione, the Italian equivalent of Intensive Care. She is very critically injured. Her blood pressure is extremely low. She has cracked ribs, a broken sternum, a collapsed lung, and a severely shattered right leg. She is paralyzed on the left side of her body and is comatose. They don't expect her to live. I'm very sorry."

My worst fears were confirmed. My mouth became dry, and my stomach churned. But at the same time, a supernatural calm invaded my mind. I found myself saying things to the doctor that only the Lord could have given me the perspective to say.

"My wife is a Christian. She has accepted Christ as her Savior. I am going to pray that God will spare her life, but if He chooses not to, I know His plan is best. If she dies, I know she will be spared the pain and suffering, and she will be in heaven with Christ."

"It's good to have faith at a time like this," the doctor responded. "If you wish, I will take you to see your wife in intensive care."

Walking, we talked about our families and the uncertainty of life and death. We spoke of not appreciating our loved ones enough until something like this happens.

I tried to prepare myself for the worst, but they would not let me see Jill. They said her condition was too serious. "Come back tomorrow," they said. "Tomorrow?" I thought. "Will she be alive tomorrow?"

It was about 10:30 p.m. as I drove home trying to focus on the road through tear-filled eyes. I cried out to God all the way home. I pleaded for her life. I was numbed by the thought of going on through life without her, raising our boys alone. We had dated since high school, almost grown up together. We had struggled through hard times financially, as we went through college and seminary. We had worked together with a full-time youth ministry at Northwest Bible Church in Dallas for six years. We had seen God supernaturally set us apart to serve as missionaries in Rome. From as far back as I could remember, it was always Dennis and Jill together—we were a team. After fourteen years of marriage, was this the end?

I dried my eyes before going up to our apartment. Nancy Weynand, a co-worker, greeted me. She had come to be with the boys. I went to their bedroom and found them in bed, but wide awake. For privacy, I took them out on our patio and closed the sliding glass door. I started out by reminding them that the Lord knows what's best for us and Mom. Then I told them the Lord may be taking her to be with Him.

Then I did what I had not done, but twice, since my father's funeral. I cried. My boys cried, too, and we each prayed. We thanked God that Jon was okay, and then asked the Lord to spare Mom if it was His will.

We never questioned our coming to Italy, because that road had been clearly marked. We went to bed, but not to sleep—uncertain as to what the daylight would bring. As I lay in bed, eyes wide open, I recalled the clear leading of God from Dallas, Texas, to Rome, Italy.

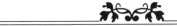

REFLECTIONS ON STRENGTH

When unanticipated strangulation of our lives takes place, our weaknesses and inability to cope loom large.

"STRENGTH: Power in general, operative energy; ability to do or hear. One regarded as an embodiment of sustaining or protecting power; in archaic or poetic use, a fortress."

Who makes strength available?

> *"The Lord is my shepherd. I shall not want…Even though I walk through the valley of the shadow of death, I fear no evil; for You are with me; Your rod and Your staff, they comfort me…Surely goodness and lovingkindness will follow me all the days of my life. And I will dwell in the house of the Lord forever."*
>
> Psalm 23:1,4,6

Does fear need to control us?

What are the functions of God's rod and staff?

In spite of trouble, what are God's promises to me?

Can we be strong when we are totally out of control of the circumstances?

> *"For man is born for trouble, as sparks fly upward. But as for me, I would seek God, And would place my cause before God; Who does great and unsearchable things, wonders without number."*
>
> Job 5:7-9

> *"In my distress, I called upon the Lord, and cried to my God for help; He heard my voice out of His temple, and my cry for help before Him came into His ears."*
>
> Psalm 18:6

How should this look daily? In response to the Lord's help, what advice are we given?

> *"Only be very careful to observe the commandment…of the Lord…to love the Lord your God and walk in all His ways and keep His commandments and hold fast to Him*

and serve Him with all your heart and with all your soul." Joshua 22:5

Describe God's almighty care in verses 2 and 3 of Psalms 18.

"The Lord is my rock and my fortress and my deliverer. My God, my rock, in whom I take refuge; my shield and the horn of my salvation, my stronghold."
Psalms 18:2-3

CHAPTER TWO

Step Right Up

by Jill

"Jill, I'd like you to come up and meet someone." My husband's voice had that "this is important" inflection. I followed my husband into his office to greet Mr. Peck with great hesitation.

The previous evening Royal Peck had spoken at our church's missions conference. He was already envisioning sending Dennis and me off to Rome, Italy to lead a team of twenty five "singles" facilitating street ministry. The group would stand on a street corner and tell people how they could personally know Jesus as their Savior.

Similarities in philosophy of ministry between my husband and Mr. Peck had been notable the evening before. I had decided I would not engage my husband in conversation regarding Mr. Peck's vision of reaching Italy for Christ. If his presentation had really grabbed Dennis' attention, I was sure Dennis would inform me of his newfound propensity.

I was a prophet. Dennis was now introducing me to Mr. Peck. His overwhelming friendliness and wide smile punctuated his desire for further, more in-depth conversation. Dennis suggested that he come to our home that night to share more about his ministry in Italy and what our possible involvement could be.

"Possible involvement!" my mind screamed. "Of course not! Oh, that couldn't be possible," I thought. I quickly excused myself and headed back to my refuge—the car. Driving home, my heart was pierced by words from a well-known hymn that began to play on the Christian radio station. Tears of anguish poured out of my confused mind. What did the Lord have in mind for us? We had never been directed toward a ministry in missions. What place of importance was this new challenge going to have in our lives? Surely it would all pass. We had never been directed towards serving in another country and carrying the dismal title of "missionaries." My mind was rambling through many questions. I needed to talk to my husband.

Mr. Royal Peck had already been a missionary for 22 years in Italy with Greater Europe Missions and was now the director of Christ's Mission. Sending teams of career-age young people to various towns in Italy to establish churches was the scope of the mission's ministry. Desiring to use the energy and enthusiasm of young adults caught my husband's attention. The Biblical principles and commitment to discipleship that Mr. Peck had presented coincided with the convictions of ministry my husband was already seeing the Lord bless.

Dallas had become home. Our two youngest sons were born here. Dennis had earned his Doctorate of Theology degree from Dallas Theological School, and we were able to buy our first home. Our first full-time ministry employment was with the Northwest Bible Church of Dallas, which we had grown to love.

The first years of marriage had been a struggle financially as my husband was finishing college, doing post-graduate work, holding down part-time jobs, and being a father. The Lord had provided for specific needs often. Finally, we were living in our own home in a nice neighborhood with dreams of household plans and decor that would provide a comfortable environment for hospitality. We had worked hard and had learned many lessons. There must be many more lessons to learn.

REFLECTIONS ON CHANGED PLANS

The Bible has a plan for our lives with God's commands and guidelines for our protection.

Is He trustworthy when His plan seems light years away from what we have ever thought or imagined?

> *"Your lovingkindness, O Lord, extends to the heavens, Your faithfulness reaches to the skies. Your righteousness is like the mountains of God; Your judgments are like a great deep..."*   Psalms 36:5-6

> *"Come now, you who say, 'Today or tomorrow we shall go to such and such a city, and spend a year there and engage in business and make a profit.' Yet you do not know what your life will be like tomorrow. You are just a vapor that appears for a little while and then vanishes away. Instead, you ought to say, 'If the Lord wills, we will live and also do this or that.' "*   James 4:13-15

Describe God's character qualities seen in these verses. What security does that bring His child?

"Do not fear, for I am with you; Do not anxiously look about you, for I am your God. I will strengthen you, surely I will help you. Surely I will uphold you with my righteous right hand."   Isaiah 41:10

Knowing our limitations as humans, why is it to our best advantage to seek God's plan for our lives?

Will obedience produce contentment?

"But godliness actually is a means of great gain, when accompanied by contentment."   I Timothy 6:6

CHAPTER THREE

A Royal Rap

by Jill

Supper had been served, and the children had been put to bed. A turmoil of inquisitive looks and comments pervaded the atmosphere as my husband and I waited for our guest's arrival. Royal Peck *did* come bustling in with his usual amount of energetic speech and enthusiasm, intending to lure our interest. He gave us a more complete picture of Italy Project 1 by telling us of a previous trial project in Rome, Italy—its successes and failures. He told of the Lord's ministry for him and his family in Italy for 22 years, and of the great burden and vision the Lord had instilled in him for team ministries in Italy. The history of Christ's Mission and how the Lord had opened his present position as director strongly demonstrated the power of God made visible to those who walk by faith. He related the great need for leaders to direct the teams of adults required to established churches in areas where there were no known believers. We would be part of the leadership group of nine people helping to administrate the ministry and living affairs of about 25 singles. Six months of language preparation in Florence would be needed before moving to Rome. The team would conduct regular street meetings in Rome, giving individual testimonies of God's work in their lives and singing Christ-centered songs to attract the attention of passers-by. Street meetings would be necessary to reach the Italians, as one cannot visit door-to-door in the apartment buildings. Access to homes is not given unless the person of the house gives permission for admittance to the building. After the street meetings, contacts would be made with those standing close by. When the person(s) desired, a weekly Bible study would then commence in their home. Whew! Would there be any time for family?

Living in apartments is the normal mode of living in Italy. Thus, we would be living in an apartment, as opposed to a house. American Overseas Schools were available for the children if funds were accessible to send them. Our meeting had been positive, friendly—and challenging.

Dennis and I began to prayerfully converse with our heavenly Father over the next few weeks and months, desirous to discern what would bring honor to Him at this point in our lives. Was it His will to uproot our family? Was it His will to forsake the familiarity of home and to be transplanted in another culture and country? What did He desire?

In the following days, we began to call our parents, brothers and sisters—asking them to join us in fervent prayer. We needed much wisdom and direction. The Lord did not seem to be negating our involvement with missions. Rather, its challenge began to be taken seriously.

The following week, as I worked in the kitchen, the stove caught my attention. It looked just like Mother's. Suddenly, I collapsed at its side in a barrage of uncontrollable tears. I would miss mother very much. I wouldn't get to be with her often if we were moving to another country. Enjoying her specialties in the kitchen which accompanied her hospitality in Kansas City would be missed by our family.

She had always been the model I followed. Mom and Dad's home held such security and comfort. The hurt was piercing deeply, and crying was the only appropriate release.

"Oh, Lord, do you love me? How can we leave the States and all our loved ones? It will be so hard to be separated and alone!" my heart cried.

"Jill, do you know what a privilege it is to have such a close relationship with godly parents who have cared for you faithfully from the time you were born? Maybe *thankfulness* is in order," the Lord prompted.

The months that followed were often filled with tearful questions and hurtful thoughts of separation. Yes, I spoke regularly with my heavenly Father letting Him speak to me through His holy word, the Bible. Even if I did not feel like talking to Him, I certainly knew that I needed to be quiet and hear what He wanted to say to me and be ready to receive His peace in my heart. Months were passing, and we had not received a definite "yes" that we were to go, but all that we could sense and observe indicated God saying, "Yes, you <u>are</u> to go!" We had come to the point of complete willingness if this was the Lord's will for us.

Yes, I was willing to cross the oceans to this far-away country if it truly was what my Lord desired. No, I did not have peace reigning in me, though I did have a submissive attitude if this was my Father's will. I was confused.

My husband had wisely given me the freedom to pray about our becoming missionaries overseas and to tell him exactly what I felt was the Lord's will. If I felt that it definitely was not of the Father, he wanted me to tell him; and he was willing to accept that as the Lord's leading. I had the freedom to yell and shout and say, "No way!" However, being a daughter of my Father, I certainly wanted to please Him. He had given me a husband to follow who loved Him as well. I did not want to stand in the way of His divine direction to my husband. I was willing, but doubtful that it would come to pass. After all, it would require a lot of miracles. However, I knew that if this was the Father's will for us, He would give me real peace in my heart. I would look for it and wait ... and wait ... and wait ... otherwise, perhaps it would not be His will.

REFLECTIONS ON FOLLOWING

God's ultimate knowledge in His timeline perspective is often a challenge to our commitment.

Does God love me when He asks something hard of me?

"And walk in love, just as Christ also loved you and gave Himself up for us, an offering and a sacrifice to God as a fragrant aroma."   Ephesians 5:2

"Who shall separate us from the love of Christ? Will tribulation, or distress, or persecution, or famine, or nakedness, or peril, or sword? ...But in all these things we overwhelmingly conquer through Him who loved us."
                    Romans 8:35,37

What discipline is He desiring to develop in me to produce strong spiritual muscles?

"We are destroying speculations and every lofty thing raised up against the knowledge of God, and we are taking every thought captive to the obedience of Christ."
II Corinthians 10:5

Can I trust Him to lead me through my husband?

"In the same way, you wives, be submissive to your own husbands so that even if any of them are disobedient to the word, they may be won without a word by the behavior of their wives, as they observe your chaste and respectful behavior...For in this way in former times the holy women also, who hoped in God, used to adorn themselves, being submissive to their own husbands."
I Peter 3:1,2,5

Why is my husband placed in authority over me?

"For the husband is the head of the wife, as Christ also is the head of the church, He Himself being the Savior of the body. But as the church is subject to Christ, so also the wives ought to be to their husbands in everything."
Ephesians 5:23-24

How are husbands asked to reflect Christ in their role as husband?

"Husbands, love your wives, just as Christ also loved the church and gave Himself up for it."
Ephesians 5:25

CHAPTER FOUR

Grow Up, Girl

by Jill

We had arrived in Kansas City to participate in my brother's wedding. A week with Mom and Dad would be energizing. I could bend their ear and get all their sympathy. I knew they would care about my present state of agony.

But who gets the attention when a wedding takes place? The bride and groom! The festivities of the week pivoted around the main characters of the gala event. Attention and conversation centered around the establishment of their new home. Time slots to relate my woes kept vanishing.

Frustrated, I would often lie in bed in the mornings reading my Father's message to me searching for some twig of assurance, some twig of hope to which I could cling. "Lord, when will I sense Your peace about moving clear around the world away from family and friends? No one here has time for me or special insight into my inner struggles. If this is Your will, Lord, please give me peace." His voice spoke clearly through my sobbing that morning. "Jill, you are no longer your parent's little girl. Rather you are a grown woman with three children. You are a wife and mother. I will give you the ability to cope with these new situations. I will endow you with the ability to handle the job I give you." His words in Joshua 1:9 rang out strong and clear, *"Be strong and courageous! Do not tremble or be dismayed, for the Lord your God is with you wherever you go."*

"Lord, You are with me wherever I go? You are with me now in Kansas City. You will be with me in Rome, Italy, as well?" His interminable presence and role reminders began to persuade embalming peace to flood my soul. I pondered His perspective. How beautiful! How freeing! Truly I was being liberated. Liberated from my own confining cells of materialism and "mamma's baby." I could see that I was functioning adequately in the responsibilities and roles the Lord had blessed me with. He would continue to enable me to function in the new role of missionary if that would serve His purposes best.

I finished dressing and gathered all of the family's paraphernalia together. We were about ready to start back to Dallas. My parents and other family members stood encircling us in the wood-paneled family room to say good-bye and to ask God's blessing upon our return trip home. I felt such peace and contentment.

The following months were filled with seeing the Father's exclamation mark behind His command, "Go!" We presented Christ's Mission's ministry and its goals for Project I in Rome, Italy, to a variety of classes and fellowship groups in the church, desiring to educate them to the Lord's direction in our lives.

The board of elders approved our going after six months of prayer and information gathering. The Missions Committee heartily endorsed our new calling as well and asked my husband Dennis to be one of the keynote speakers at their missions conference in February.

That particular conference was culminated by the congregation voting to grant us full support financially to be a part of the church-planting project in Italy! Our hearts were filled with awe to watch Him work! We praised and thanked Him.

A short time later, Dennis left to spend a month in Europe with Mr. Royal Peck, the director of the mission. Observations could be made in regard to the team ministry and the zone in which they would be working. He could become familiar with the new culture where he would bring his family and be ministering.

The weeks dragged heavily. I felt very alone. Much activity had passed with more adventure in store.

I did not receive any mail from Europe, waiting anxiously for news from my husband. Hearing his impressions and the particulars of what he had seen was important to me. His secretary and others would call and say that they had received a note from him and wanted to pass his comments along to me. Not a word came. Ugh! I was upset and bothered. Characteristically, I would hear from him first. A postcard had not even arrived.

Soundly I was sleeping one night, when suddenly the phone rang. I had to shake myself to try to awaken to answer. Finally, I reached from the bed, lifted the receiver to my ear and heard a loving, familiar voice. Hearing Dennis' voice forced my mind to work to comprehend all he was saying and to interact intelligently. Yes, he had written me several times right from the beginning of the trip and was surprised that the letters had not been delivered. He was learning pertinent information about our new frontier, but was eager to come home. After our last good-bye, I forced myself to remain awake to think through all of our conversation so that I could remember in the morning. Soon he would be home.

REFLECTIONS ON FREEDOM

Christ teaches He is the vine, and we are the branches in John 15. Sometimes I feel like a twig. *"Thus says the Lord God, 'I will also take a sprig from the lofty top of the cedar and set it out; I will pluck from the topmost of its young twigs a tender one and I will plant it on a high and lofty mountain.' "* Ezekiel 17:22. **The Lord says He will plant the twig on a high and lofty mountain!**

Does God's presence with His child prompt her to be strong and courageous?

> *"Hear my prayer, O Lord, Give ear to my supplications! Answer me in Thy faithfulness, in Thy righteousness!...my spirit is overwhelmed within me; my heart is appalled within me...Teach me to do Thy will, for Thou art my God..."*   Psalm 143:1,4,10

Has His Word, the Bible, embalmed your soul with His peace recently?

> *"Let the peace of Christ rule in your hearts, to which indeed you were called in one body; and be thankful. Let the word of Christ richly dwell within you..."*
> Colossians 3:15-16a

Do you need to be liberated from something that keeps you from following God's will for your life?

> *"...we too all formerly lived in the lusts of our flesh, indulging the desires of the flesh and of the mind, and were by nature children of wrath, even as the rest. But God, being rich in mercy, because of His great love with which He loved us, even when we were dead in our transgressions, made us alive together with Christ (by grace you have been saved.)"*   Ephesians 2:3-5

> *"In Him we have redemption through His blood, the forgiveness of our trespasses, according to the riches of His grace."*   Ephesians 1:7

Have you seen God's faithfulness in the past?

Does He give you the ability to respond properly?

> *"Now those who belong to Christ Jesus have crucified the flesh with its passions and desires. If we live by the Spirit, let us also walk by the Spirit."*
> Galatians 5:24-25

> *"But the fruit of the Spirit is love, joy, peace, patience, kindness, goodness, faithfulness, gentleness, self-control; against such things there is no law."*
> Galatians 5:22-23

What has He asked of you in the roles that you fill?

> *"To sum up, all of you be harmonious, sympathetic, brotherly, kindhearted, and humble in spirit; not returning evil for evil or insult for insult, but giving a blessing instead; for you were called for the very purpose that you might inherit a blessing."*   I Peter 3:8,9

For further study, one could see Titus 2:3-5

Are you good at following orders?

CHAPTER FIVE

Sell, Store or Pack?

by Jill

A myriad of details required tackling for moving preparation when Dennis returned. All of our clothes, linens, kitchen utensils and other essential items needed to be packed. In every category, we had to determine what we must sell, store or take. Decision-making seemed endless. Some items we were told would not be appropriate. One couldn't be sure, either, how the electrical appliances would perform. Transformers were essential. Would there be adequate electricity? Our two oldest sons, ages 10 and 8, hated to part with their nice bedroom furniture. Their large room had one wall artistically painted with their names, Tod and Scot, several feet high on a blue sweeping panel. The personalized decor had captured their young hearts. Leaving our very first home, as it screamed out their names, would be too difficult!

Bedside conversations occasionally brought tears and questions. "Why do we have to go?" "Why must we move?" "Where will we live?" "Who will be our friends?" "Will there be football teams?" "I'll miss Chad." Chad was their very good friend down the block.

Listening to their feelings of woe was very important, as well as not responding critically to their childlike assessment of the "big move." I shared, as well, some of our own fears and dislike of change—but punctuated it by our commitment to obey what our heavenly Father was showing us to do. The Lord had taken care of us in the past and He would continue to care for us in the future. In the midst of all the questions and disruptive changes, children can still feel secure as they are assured of their parents' love, care and understanding. We did have prayer together, talking to God about all our concerns and asking Him for peace. Tender moments of goodnight kisses followed.

I began to work my way through closets and drawers, determining what should be sold at my garage sale, what should be packed for future use or what items could be stored in one of the closets. The items for a good-sized garage sale grew. Having to part with furniture was so difficult. Storage would be too costly. Alas, what would we have in Italy? Only the Father knew.

A couple of months before our move to New Jersey, where the Mission headquarters was located, we told our good friend and Realtor Jack Coats that we would like to rent our home to a seminary couple, should he learn of someone with that particular need. Dennis' brother would care for the house while we were gone. Not too many days had passed when we received a phone call from Jack. "An incoming seminary student is interested in renting a home for his wife and two sons for the next five years. He has chosen to be a part of the five-year program at seminary. Can he come over and see the place?" Not only had our Father brought us renters for the specific five years we would be gone, but they had also decided on an affordable monthly payment that coincided precisely with the monthly rate we were asking! The payments during our five-year absence on Italy Project I would be covered by a family we could trust at the very amount needed. What a great God! What a wonderful Father! He was taking good care of us. *"If you consent and obey, you will eat the best of the land."* Isaiah 1:19 *"Behold, God is my salvation, I will trust and not be afraid."* Isaiah 12:2

Household belongings had all been packed, labeled, and loaded into our rented trailer. Packing for vacation time in Virginia, packing for basic needs in New Jersey and Florence, and packing for Rome kept us always in need of more boxes and more suitcases. A friend from church and her companion came to the house and started scrubbing floors and bathrooms from top to bottom. I was still packing last-minute trivia while they busily cleaned. They worked hard with attitudes pleased to help. Their efforts allowed me the pleasure of leaving a clean house in good shape much earlier in the day than otherwise would have been possible. The following week we stayed with a family in the church who had opened their home for our convenience.

Jill's Journal:

June 1, 1979

The Sewells have been our hosts this past week and have been excellent!

I especially enjoyed a few moments' rest on the hammock with a refreshing limeade Ann served me. Fred stayed up 'til late making sure the trailer was packed soundly and was in good shape as a father would.

I gave Ann a plaque that perfectly described my feelings; "Lord, the sea is so great, and my boat is so small." God, thank you for our friends. Thank you for our family.

The morning that we began our trip to New Jersey, they saw us off in a very parental manner, taking care to note little needs.

Our ultimate destination was Clifton, New Jersey, where we would rent a church-owned house designated for missionaries. In route, however, we would enjoy the scenery to Roanoke, Virginia and visit Dennis' brother who pastored the Calvary Memorial Church. Spending time together with family members was extra special. We enjoyed good times of laughter, picnics, fishing and games 'til late.

The final leg of our trip seemed to come too quickly. We had wanted to arrive in Clifton while it was still light. First, however, we had to go to Christ's Mission headquarters in Hackensack and be given the address and directions. By the time we reached the house, of course, the sun had set.

Several mission staff members had come to the house earlier to prepare a proper welcome for us. The living room had a big white sign saying, "Welcome." Various personal touches showed that someone cared. They had cared enough to put fresh breakfast groceries in the refrigerator, which we greatly appreciated the following morning. The home had been well cared for and included a nicely equipped kitchen, linens and a perfect large bedroom area for the boys upstairs. We were being taken care of very well.

Thank you, Father.

June 17, 1979

Our first Sunday as residents in Clifton, New Jersey, happened to be Father's Day. Being a visitor in a new place, at a new church, can make one feel awkward. This past week of getting settled has been just a slight struggle as I have found myself between the tug of two feelings: One part of me wanting to cry, wishing I weren't here at all and another part saying, "Be objective. Things are really nice here if you will be patient to see them that way." My moods portray what I see out the window. A ray of sunshine brings cheer and familiarity of where I've been. Clouded sunshine reminds me of where I am.

A battle disrupts inside me as I try to hold on to Dallas ways, its fashions, its talk, its social life and standards. I want to be identified with them. Knowing, too, our stay here will be six to nine months makes it more difficult to want to embrace the culture here. Probably, it is mostly psychological. Again, I need to live each day for the opportunities God brings me—not look too far into the future.

The driving here is probably the most difficult item to become accustomed to. It truly seems maniacal—whizzing in and out as though every destination was an emergency. I'm trusting God to be with me in my travel on these highways. My guardian angel will be kept busy.

Many personal items have been unpacked to make us feel more at home. It helps to see a familiar washcloth, a picture or plate. I've also enjoyed the gifts people gave me reminding me of the friends and love God has blessed us with in the past. He is faithful. He is the same God here as the one I worshipped and marveled at in Texas. He is with me. The trees and lovely flowers so abundant here are His creation and provision for me to feel at home. This is my Father's world. His handiwork makes me feel more at home.

June 18, 1979
Wednesday morning we arose early to get ready for a

family visit to Christ's Mission. Mr. Peck invited us to come and share with the staff and participate in their prayer time. Yes, we did feel like strangers sitting in a neat row among all the staff members.

I briefly shared a few of God's abounding provisions though my tired brain didn't seem to cooperate in giving anything too deep or meaningful. Dennis shared a few thoughts on dying to self from Romans. The boys entered in answering questions about their expectations. Then Mr. Peck announced the basis for postponing staff training for Project I—namely $54,000 needed. Some significant changes and decisions have to be made accordingly. All the arrangements we made for the children's care with grandparents during that time will have to be altered. Our own coming could have been delayed and our vacation extended. Disappointments!

The boys, Dennis and I have been playing badminton as a family diversion from the constant reminders of our new surroundings. We are such creatures of habit, resisting change. Every first time experience seems to leave a lump in my throat or at least tempt one into coming—whether it's doing the laundry, finding a workable arrangement in the living room or visiting a new church.

Sunday morning was bright with sunshine. Happily I got ready, anxious to be able to sit and drink in God's Word. I needed it! The radio was playing hymns loud enough to infect our whole family with preparation to receive God's Word.

The nursery worker cheerily received Jon. Another man volunteered to escort Tod and Scot to their classes. Dennis and I walked toward the class to which we had been guided. There was no introduction or mention of visitors. Our home church at least recognized and made an effort to welcome guests. The teacher, a young man, was apparently teaching church history. Afterwards, no one bothered to say hello or to find out anything about us except another visiting couple—who were missionaries!

A wave of bitterness was creeping up inside the lump in my throat. I wanted to be recognized. Here we were—all the way from Dallas, having left a nice home, a large church, and sunny skies. Doesn't anyone care? We're here!

Yes, it was Father's Day and I could barely muster a smile for my husband. We didn't meet anyone—not even the family having us to their home for dinner. After returning to our house, they called and gave directions. We walked over a block and met the family.

Rain brought the ham picnic to an abrupt close. After coffee, the husband excused himself to work on a proposal due the next morning. We had dessert and walked back home.

Scot wanted to go back to the church that evening as he had made two friends. For some strange reason, I felt I had to go back, too. I knew why after the first hymn.

Make Me A Captive, Lord
Matheson Hustad

1. Make me a captive, Lord,
   And then I shall be free;
   Force me to render up my sword,
   And I shall conqueror be;
   I sink in life's alarms
   When by myself I stand;

Imprison me within Thine arms,
And strong shall be my hand.

2. My heart is weak and poor
Until its Master finds;
It has no spring of action sure.
It varies with the wind,
It cannot freely move
'Till Thou has wrought its chain;
Enslave it with Thy matchless love,
And deathless it shall reign.

3. My power is faint and low
'Till I have learned to serve:
It wants the needed fire to glow,
It wants the breeze to nerve;
It cannot drive the world
Until itself be driven;
Its flag can only be unfurled
When Thou shalt breathe from
heaven.

4. My will is not my own
Till Thou has made it Thine;
If it would reach the monarch's throne,
It must its crown resign:
It only stands unbent
Amid the clashing strife,
When on Thy bosom it has leaned,
And found in Thee its life.

It spoke directly to me, and it was new. I had never sung it before. The hymn talked about being totally conquered by Christ to experience total freedom. That is what I needed: to be reminded of being alive to Christ and dead to self.

Glorify Him through the opportunities He gives you today. Put down your defense mechanisms and let Christ conquer all through you. *"But one thing I do: forgetting what lies behind and reaching forward to what lies ahead, I press on toward the goal for the prize of the upward call of God in Christ Jesus."* Philippians 3:13b, 14

I need to "forget" and not compare unfavorably everyone and everything new I encounter. Thoughts of Dallas cannot consume my time, nor the glory of past successes. I must reach forward to the lives God wants us to touch here, today. Miracles and lessons He has planned for us now as we watch Him work, preparing our team for Italy. *"However, let us keep living by the same standard to which we have attained."*

Philippians 3:16. Comfort came to me as I read this. Perhaps I have not textually interpreted it correctly, but right now it helps me to think I can still be me. The standards for entertaining and keeping my home nice and looking well-groomed don't have to alter.

The "me" God has developed all these years is who I am. Use me for His glory. Benefit from the good things of the past to make them beneficial for the present.

"Lord, create in me a clean heart. Use me today to honor Your Son, my Savior. Help me reach out to Barbara and Ben who are across the street. They have been friendly and open. Thank You for Your work here." I got up this morning in time to pack Dennis a lunch and fix him breakfast. We had prayer together. It's his first day to work at Christ's Mission.

He said to me last night, "Remember, I didn't bring us here. God did." He doesn't want credit for it. I think he misses home, too. When I called him at work, he was busy moving boxes of books out of a room that was to become his office.

Jon reminds me at least once a day, "I'm ready to move ..." referring to going back home. Every time he wakes up, he comments that this really isn't his room or his bed. I hope his toys arrive soon.

The screened-in front porch where I'm sitting is perfectly cheery. The geraniums I purchased yesterday add a little zest. God has blessed us in another way by providing a run-down mini-bike for the boys to ride. The cleaning and repairing has been a good work project for them as they look forward to the rewards of their work. A friend from Christ's Mission brought it for them as her neighbor was giving it away. Just an added blessing. God deserves our praise.

June 21, 1979

Dennis came home from the mission late, tired, covered with paint from head to toe and dismayed. He had met with the Mission directors. Several of their decisions brought personal disappointment.

I know God wants us to be receptive to pressure He allows. I pray our response would be one of submissiveness, and acceptance of circumstances from God—not blaming individuals involved. It is hard to make the transition from being at the church to being at the mission. Dennis will have to purchase his own paper and a typewriter. I think I will be his secretary soon here at home.

June 29, 1979

Last evening, Corrie ten Boom's life story was shown at the church. It was my second time to view it and, by far, the most meaningful. I was reminded of the spiritual warfare we are in. As Christians, our cross should be carried daily—open homes to the needy means open hearts. I felt moved to make this one of my goals—to put my self-interests aside for the people's needs. God gave me a good opportunity to do just that!

Barbara, our neighbor across the street, visited with me for a while on the sidewalk. I had brought Jon over to play with her five-year-old Douglas. She began asking me questions, relating that she had a Catholic friend who had become "born again." Was I one of those people called "born again?" The Lord opened a beautiful opportunity to share how one could be born again in Jesus Christ. I certainly don't feel that I smoothly uttered forth all the right words. God is the One to work in her heart. I hope she can come to understand Christ's love for her better as she observes me. I invited her to bring Douglas to the church's Camp Character running through the summer and attend a ladies' Bible class with me. She would love to! We will alternate driving.

July 4, 1979

Moving is hard. It's finally all catching up with me. I'm having difficulty finding anything to make me smile. I look for some tiny remembrance of home and am disappointed I can't find it. Today is a holiday and normally one thinks of sunshine, family, and fireworks at the Cotton Bowl. We all cleaned the house and got ready to go to a small town fair. But it started raining and is very cold. We had to wear jackets. Dennis was trying hard to cheer us up and drove to Mario's for pizza.

I miss my friends, neighbors, community shops, stores, pretty streets, blue skies, sunshine, white clouds, people smiling, social graces, my baby grand piano, laying out in the sun, quiet streets, our pretty creek, the children's friends, and all our church family at Northwest Bible Church.

I feel imprisoned here—by people, roads, the mission, and gray skies.

"I need Thee every hour."

REFLECTIONS ON GOD'S GIFT

Strangling Christ-like actions and responses is the evil one's goal.

When one feels imprisoned, who can he/she turn to?

"See to it that no one takes you captive through philosophy and empty deception, according to the tradition of men, according to the elementary principles of the world, rather than according to Christ. For in Him all the fullness of Deity dwells in bodily form."

Colossians 2:8-9

If Jesus is God, why did He come to earth as a human?

"Have this attitude in yourselves which was also in Christ Jesus, who although He existed in the form of God, did

not regard equality with God a thing to be grasped, but emptied Himself, taking the form of a bond-servant, and being made in the likeness of men. Being found in appearance as a man, He humbled Himself by becoming obedient to the point of death, even death on a cross."
Philippians 2:5-8

Why did Christ have to die?

"For all have sinned and come short of the glory of God."
Romans 3:23

"For the wages of sin is death, but the free gift of God is eternal life in Christ Jesus our Lord." Romans 6:23

How can God's gift be free? What can I do to earn it?

"For by grace you have been saved through faith; and that not of yourselves, it is the gift of God; not as a result of works, so that no one might boast."
Ephesians 2:8-9

If I can't do enough good works to merit salvation, how can I become God's child?

"That if you confess with your mouth Jesus as Lord, and believe in your heart that God raised Him from the dead, you shall be saved; for with the heart a person believes, resulting in righteousness, and with the mouth he confesses, resulting in salvation." Romans 10:9-10

How can I know Jesus Christ better and understand what He wants me to do?

> *"And I will ask the Father, and He will give you another Helper that He may be with you forever, that is the Spirit of truth...He will teach you all things and bring to your remembrance all that I said to you."*
> John 14:16,17a,26b

Are you saying that the Holy Spirit comes to indwell me when I confess my sin and invite Jesus into my heart?

> *"Because you are sons, God has sent forth the Spirit of His Son into our hearts, crying 'Abba!' (literally 'daddy') Father!'"*
> Galatians 4:6

Do your past failures have to defeat you or can you be purposed to follow Christ with each moment?

> *"Do not call to mind the former things, or ponder things of the past. Behold, I will do something new..."*
> Isaiah 43:18,19a

Is a lifestyle change needed?

> *"Therefore do not let sin reign in your mortal body so that you should obey its lusts...but present yourselves to God as those alive from the dead, and your members as instruments of righteousness to God."*
> Romans 6:12-13

What response is honoring to Christ when disappointments loom large?

> *"Be anxious for nothing, but in everything by prayer and supplication with thanksgiving let your requests be make known to God."* Philippians 4:6

CHAPTER SIX

Coping With Comparisons

by Jill

Scot asked the other day if possibly he and Tod could live with a friend in Dallas, go to school there and come home for the holidays!

July 27, 1979

Tonight ends another saga of homesickness. My day was well spent trotting from one errand to the next looking crisp and coiffured. But somehow around supper time, reflections on my "market circuit" lulled my mind into acknowledging the knot in my stomach called homesickness. I had set foot in my first department store in New Jersey. How I longed to run to my "own" special bargain places where they knew me—and I knew what they carried.

July 28, 1979

Last night we all viewed the familiar skyline of "Big D" via the program, "Dallas"—and all expressed that sweet longing for the familiar! The passageways I have driven on a million times made me long to go home. Though, as I told the children, I never want to be in Dallas 'til I know God wants me there. Above all, I want to please Him. My dear husband recognized God's hand in leading our family— not the director of the mission. God's will is priority—our major goal is to obey Him.

<u>August 14, 1979</u>

After work a few days ago, we started driving to Chicago to visit Evelyn and Erwin Lange, Dennis' mother and step-father. We were excited to have a change from our unfamiliar new surroundings. Instead, however, a gloom passed over me for intangible reasons. Perhaps I was concerned how relatives would relate to our new role as "missionaries", especially Dennis' grandmother! She would not see us as weird. She would be full of joy and thankfulness for the great pleasure we would have in becoming missionaries. Obedience to God always brings joy—right? I didn't feel joyful. Matching her joy would be a challenge, but one I knew God would bring in His own time. Her joy and thanksgiving would be hard to match—hard to tame. Right now I *do not* feel joyful and I do not want to have to *act* joyful! I know God will change that, but I don't know what His timing will be. I struggle with how others see my new role, which probably is ultimately concerned with how *I* see my new role.

The turning point of my agony, however, was transformed into joy by the very woman whose joy I did not think I could match—Dennis' grandmother now living in a nursing home. At 85, she looked bright-eyed with a forever smile—face framed by cloud-like curls, soft and billowy. This lady stood out! From a distance we got our first glimpse of her silhouette framed in the dusk-lit hallway. Two elderly folks faced each other in wheel chairs engaging in lively conversation. The one on the left began to deftly wheel toward us. She seemed a sight of perfect health amongst the ruins of people.

Amidst the greetings and usual clamor, she asked knowingly, "Jill, are you homesick? I've felt strongly that you were, and I've been praying over and over for you. My dear child," she whispered as I acknowledged her keen sensitivity, "I'll pray, but I know it is hard. It's always hard to crucify the flesh."

There it was. She had said it—the empathetic, prayerful appraisal I was seeking! Someone to know. Someone to understand. She knew. She understood. The years of time had not separated her from knowing God in His fullness, from perceiving the daily dying of self we all must succumb to if the resurrected life, the new creature, is to be identified, fruitful.

Her mission field has been the nursing home. No, she didn't ask to have the ailments that placed her there, to lose her mate, to dine on cafeteria food while urine odors wafted occasionally through each chamber, or to have senility sharing her surroundings with whines and groans too stark to be forgotten.

Yet, she believes God placed her there. A count of 59 persons who have trusted Jesus as their Savior are her crown. Her Bible, cover worn and tattered, is leafed through with regularity. Women come to this strong Dutch woman to receive insight into the Holy Scriptures.

None of us ever get too old to serve Jesus—to learn of Him. Humbly, our knees shall bow before His glorious majesty. Age of soul blooms beautiful with youthful vigor and mature wisdom.

"Lord, never let me put myself on a shelf and write, 'It is finished,' when you never have."

Kissing and hugging the strong, round frame, shedding tears along the way, her great grandsons wheeled her to the door to say their last good-bye. "God bless you."

Somewhat unveiling my feelings, healing began to take place in light of the new day. They had lovingly received us, listening to our qualms. Thus, I began to feel a joy and peace of lighthearted summer days enveloping my soul.

August 21, 1979 -

Being away was good for me, freeing me up to gain perspective of all the summer changes and adjustments. I could be myself. I felt young, vibrant and so happy. Even Dennis commented favorably on my suddenly acquired light-hearted spirit.

Haunting me in the back shadows of my mind was: "Will I fall to pieces when we leave Chicago or when we arrive home in New Jersey?" I was enjoying my spirit soaring gleefully ahead and not dwelling pitifully on my recent entourage of unpleasant experiences. No, I don't want that to happen. I don't wish to ever feel the weight of that heavy, heartsick pity.

By God's grace, I have said good-bye to it. Each day, with tasks that will count for eternity, He fulfills me.

This past Saturday was particularly special. Rising early enough to stir up a batch of pancakes for the family before the boys had football practice, I quickly dressed in my tennis gear and rode along.

Though misty and dreary these August skies, Dennis and I enjoyed a game of tennis. Finishing our fiasco at the courts, we hunted for a health food store and a sports store. Returning to the car, my husband headed for a florist's shop and brought out a lovely bouquet for me. A lovely memory. A lovely morning. Spirits united, hearts aflame, warring not, but preferring one another. God's Word teaches truth for happiness in marriage: love built on a firm foundation.

Grandma Van Gorp sent the following poem to us as a special gift.

He Chose This Path For Thee

He Chose This Path For Thee, He chose this path for thee,—
No feeble chance, nor hard, relentless fate;

But love—His love hath placed thy footsteps here;
He knew the way was rough and desolate—
Knew how thy heart would often sink with fear,
Yet tenderly He whispered, "Child, I see
This path is best for thee."

He chose this path for thee,
Though well He knew sharp thorns would tear thy feet,

Knew how the brambles would obstruct the way,
Knew all the hidden dangers thou wouldst meet,
Knew how thy faith would falter day by day,
And still the whisper echoed, "Yes, I see."
This path is best for thee."

He chose this path for thee,
And well He knew that thou must tread alone

Its gloomy vales, and ford each flowing stream;
Knew how thy bleeding heart would sobbing moan,
"Dear Lord, to wake and find it all a dream, "
Love scanned it all, yet still could say, "I see
This path is best for thee."

He chose this path for thee,—
E'en while He knew the fearful midnight gloom

Thy timid shrinking soul must travel through;
How towering rocks would oft before thee loom,
And phantoms grim would meet thy frightened
view;
Still comes the whisper, "My beloved, I see
This path is best for thee."

He chose this path for thee—
What need'st thou more: This sweeter truth to
know
That, all along these strange bewildering ways,
O'er rocky steeps, and where dark rivers flow,

His loving arms will bear thee "all the days."

A few steps more, and thou thyself shalt see
This path is best for thee.

REFLECTIONS ON REJOICING

Joy's secret in the midst of circumstances was aptly stated by Nehemiah. "...For the joy of the Lord is your strength..." Nehemiah 8:10 What brings Him joy?

When one has no control over circumstances, what response does the Lord ask of us?

"Rejoice in the Lord always; again I will say, rejoice! Let your forbearing spirit be known to all men. The Lord is near."   Philippians 4:4-5

From these verses, who is our focus of joy?

What attitude needs to develop within us?

What promise envelopes these verses?

Our flesh holds onto the habit of living independently of God. Therefore, dying to self is a tough daily chore. Why is this necessary and how is it accomplished?

"...I urge you therefore, brethren, by the mercies of God, to present your bodies a living and holy sacrifice, acceptable to God, which is your spiritual service of worship. And do not be conformed to this world, but be transformed by the renewing of your mind, so that you may prove what the will of God is, that which is good and acceptable and perfect."   Romans 12:1-2

What choice must I make when my mind is filled with turmoil?

"I would have despaired unless I had believed that I would see the goodness of the Lord in the land of the living. Wait for the Lord..."   Psalms 27:13-14a

What role do older, more mature women play in our roles in womanhood today?

"Older women likewise are to be reverent in their behavior, not malicious gossips nor enslaved to much wine, teaching what is good, so that they may encourage

*the young women to love their husbands, to love their
children, to be sensible, pure, workers at home, kind,
being subject to their own husbands, so that the word of
God will not be dishonored."*   Titus 2:3-5

Can you seek out someone more mature to encourage you
in God's ways?

Who can you mentor and encourage in Jesus Christ?

CHAPTER SEVEN

New Perspectives
by Jill

August 25, 1979

I have been studying in Isaiah. Once Isaiah saw the absolute majestic holiness of God, His perfection and unmatched glory, did he feel utterly helpless and unclean before the Lord? Total unworthiness encompassed him as he saw who God is—and himself as he really was.

With that proper perspective, he was willing to accomplish the task God had for him—even though its strongest point would be marked by failure.

Sometimes I feel we may be heading full force into a ministry of futility. Obedience then becomes the only earmark of success.

"Welcome, my child, to a new world. Yes, it's also part of my creation." Shielded now I am from light-brightness of sunny skies dotted with fleecy clouds, warm smiles offering an "everyday" greeting, and residential rows recently sected by cedar fence posts. I am seeking to welcome my new surroundings and see its potential from *God's* perspective.

Across the river rises New York City, a city literally overrun by people saturated with society's stagnant heritage produced by social maladies, torments and abuse. Gray skies hover close.

I'm torn to turn away, not see what lies too close to my doorstep. Yesterdays of golden sun and laughter lure my mind away from facing raw realities.

Ever since we returned from Chicago, I have been facing common "new living" problems with new perspective and new appreciation for God's placing us here. His principles can instill joy in life in the midst of sorrow. Take them, each one, and turn them into a blessing. When a clerk is rude, I stop and pray for that person rather than let it totally drag me under. This response helped me in a practical way. I felt more positive, caring and even cared for!

One thing, however, bothered me. I also came back not wanting to have anything to do with Barbara, my neighbor. For a week, I did not talk with her, though I was extremely puzzled. In writing about the problem to our pastor's wife, I began to recognize the *root* of my difficulty. I was *afraid of failure:* afraid that I would never help her to know Christ as her Savior.

"Maybe, Lord, I don't believe you can do it—or will ever use me that way. I feel such a need for a confirmation from You, Father, to see that I am a healthy enough branch to help produce new life. Though You alone can produce Yourself in a person's life, I want to bear good fruit."

Upon recognition of my basic problem, I looked it in the eye facing it squarely and said, "Fear, you are not going to control me and keep me from being useful to my Master!" Satan's clever plot failed.

New Light

New face,
New place,
Not theirs, 'tis mine.
Alone—
With family faces near.

My husband has his work;
The children have their play,
And I have them.

No callers call.
No friends stop by.

I'd forgotten the pain of an address change:
11633, to 9.
Colmar Street became Hazelview.
Significant the arrangement of numbers
and names.

A veteran mover, I thought,
But 10 years of roots penetrate deep.
The soils of my heart resist feeding on their
new environment.

I see the moon,
The golden moon;
A shimmery sliver outside my window tells
me of
One very close.
He's here! My God is here!

Where can I go that He is not always
"here"?
Neither height, nor depth,
Nor states, nor cities,
Nor friends, nor streets

Can separate me from His love.

God's moonchild beams bright;
God's earthchild shines, too.
Light for the child.
The child for light.

August 31, 1979

I have already shared earlier my concern for Barbara and Ben—and my fear of failure. Once I recognized it, I wasn't about to let the enemy win with his subtle tricks. But I also had to recognize that maybe my will for me was not God's.

"Lord, maybe you don't desire to accomplish their salvation through me. Possibly it's a selfish desire to want so desperately for you to use me in that way. If so, use me however you see fit in my relationship with them. Let me be satisfied with what you want to do through me. I so want to be available and ready to do what you tell me."

Friday after taking the boys to school, I invited Barb in for coffee. We talked 'til 11:30 a.m. The last half an hour was most significant. As we conversed, she said she wanted to know more about our religion. She expressed definite interest and wanted to be able to make her own choice.

Barbara and her family decided to come visit our church on Sunday and to have dinner with us.

September 22, 1979

Wednesday, Barbara and I had our first Bible study together, studying the first three chapters of John. Barbara's heart is open and responsive to God's Word. We read and discussed the paragraphs. She had some good insights. She feels she needs to know more before she can trust Jesus

Christ as her Savior. One exciting comment she made was, "Jill, when you're in Italy, you must tell the people this; God's Word never changes."

October 13, 1979

A couple from the mission has agreed to care for Tod and Scot while we will be at team training. Because they have a new baby, we will be taking our youngest to Mother's in Kansas City.

The Bible study with Barb has been going so well. It's amazing to note her insights and full acceptance of God's Word as authority. In the Newcomer's Class with the pastor, she spoke out on a particular church issue, quoting Scripture we'd been studying!

A couple of weeks ago, we talked more in depth about areas bothering her. This is good to relate to real life and to build a broader base of friendship. She was so close to accepting Christ as her Savior. I feverishly went through the passages and tearfully told her how excited I will be to know when she accepts Christ.

She's afraid she won't be able to quit smoking—and she'll expect to and feels Christ will expect her to—and she won't be able to quit. Last time Barbara shared how she almost accepted Christ in Sunday School when they were going around the class and sharing their testimonies about becoming God's child. She prayed, "I may have to accept you now, Lord, to get me out of this!"

October 19, 1979

I must relate an incident that happened to our eight-year-old. While washing clothes, I heard, "Mom, can I talk to you? Something's bothering me."

"Sure."

"At school today, I pushed a boy. He hurt his leg, but when the teacher asked me about it, I told her it was an accident. But...really, I did it on purpose. I knew she'd believe me...and I didn't want her to think bad of me."

"Why did you push him?"

"He wasn't supposed to be in the restroom—there were too many. What should I do? I can't get it out of my mind."

To see the Holy Spirit at work in this tender, young heart provided nourishment and praise for my own soul. As we talked, I encouraged him to talk to the Lord about it and confess—and then admit his wrong to the teacher the following day, and ask her forgiveness.

The following day, his toothy grin beaming widely, Scot related how he'd prayed for just the right time to talk to his teacher—and how she had forgiven him. God is building character blocks in my children. I thank Him for trials and victories.

A demonstrative act of God's sovereignty and care happened this past week. A pilot from my father's church was able to fly Jon and me to Kansas City on their luxurious corporate jet. What timing! It saved us $235—and the trip was a necessity. I will leave Jon with Mom and then go back for team training. Being home with Mom and Dad for a few days is a real treat.

Jon has been quite excited about coming to Kansas City. I bought him a Hulk costume for Halloween. He was excited to be with my youngest brother, Steve. But thinking it all over, he said, "Tell me, how come I'm going to Kansas City anyway?"

October 23, 1979

Two days 'til I say good-bye to my lover: blonde hair, blue eyes and three years old. It's difficult to stop playing the "Mother" song on the finely tuned strings of my heart when the melody of love and laughter lingers on.

Mother and Dad will take excellent care of him, providing love, talks, warm hugs and a listening ear. But I can almost see the strain he feels, knowing I'm leaving for a time. The special awareness a mommy senses of needs and of tenderness deals me a certain blow in its deprivation. May the Lord wrap His strong arms of security around little Jon, giving a smile to his face, and a child-like faith that knows all is well. Jesus and Jon go hand-in-hand.

October 26, 1979

Returned from Kansas City yesterday afternoon and learned that Barbara asked Jesus to come and live in her on Wednesday in the morning. Praise our God! She had a bad cold, but had gone the night before to play Bingo. A couple of friends had decided not to return the extra card they had been given for which they hadn't paid. Barbara felt uncomfortable and different from them. The next morning laying in bed, she decided to invite Christ into her life. She started thinking about something else and realized Satan was diverting her attention. She stopped, began thinking and praying and invited Christ to be her Savior. She prayed, "I have some good points, but a lot of weak ones, too. If You want to come in, I'll do my best for You, but You have to do the rest." A life of faith begins.

God is at work in her husband Ben's life, too. He prayed on Sunday for the first time in his life, asking God to help him understand who He is. Every evening he's reading Basic Christianity by John Stott and his Living Bible.

Leaving Jon was hard, though I wouldn't let myself think about it too strongly. I gave him a calendar he can put stars on each day 'til time to come home. One thing he said was, "Can I come home when I'm still three—and then I'll turn four?" I assured him he'd come home when he was still three.

Arriving at La Guardia yesterday, my husband presented me with pink carnations. We enjoyed catching up on all the news. He handled meals and all quite well.

Tod and Scot were home from school when we pulled in the drive. Meeting them with hugs and kisses, we proceeded to celebrate Scot's ninth birthday.

After this happy occasion, however, Scot became tearful and needed to talk. His brother Jon's absence, along with my husband and I leaving for team training soon, seemed too much for him to handle. Rubbing his back seemed to help while we talked. God, love these children!

"Lord, be with the boys. I hurt for Scot's longing look. Father, be with him. Comfort him. Give little Jon a safe trip home Friday. Help Tod. Though he acts strong on the outside, he may not feel so strong on the inside. Bless them, each one. Thank you."

REFLECTIONS ON OBEDIENCE

Obedience to Christ is the earmark of success.

Isaiah was struck by God's majestic holiness. How did he suddenly see himself in comparison?

> *"...I saw the Lord sitting on a throne, lofty and exalted, with the train of his robe filling the temple. Seraphim stood above Him...And one called out to another, 'Holy, holy, holy is the Lord of hosts, the whole earth is full of His glory'...Then I said, 'Woe is me, for I am ruined! Because I am a man of unclean lips, and I live among a people of unclean lips...'"*   Isaiah 6:1-5

How do you see yourself in comparison?

Do our lips ever get us into trouble?

What was David's response?

> *"Set a guard, O Lord, over my mouth; keep watch over the door of my lips."*   Psalm 141:3

What gives birth to that which comes out of our mouths?

> *"...For the mouth speaks out of that which fills the heart."*   Matthew 12:34

What principles in Solomon's wisdom does he teach us?

"The wise in heart will be called discerning, and sweetness of speech increases persuasiveness." Proverbs 16:21

"The heart of the wise teaches his mouth, and adds persuasiveness to his lips."   Proverbs 16:21

Obedience strikes the chord of God's heart. He may be the only One to see what actually transpires in your heart as well as the results. God allows circumstances we don't like and don't understand. Have you ever felt God was asking you to do something futile, not worthy of your effort? Give an example.

How can sorrow be turned into joy? How do we benefit?

"Consider it all joy, my brethren, when you encounter various trials, knowing that the testing of your faith produces endurance. And let endurance have its perfect result, so that you may be perfect and complete, lacking in nothing. But if any of you lacks wisdom, let him ask of God, who gives to all generously and without reproach, and it will be given to him."   James 1:2-5

What's in God's directive for His children sharing Christ with others?

What's in the principle message of the gospel?

"For God so loved the world that he gave his only begotten Son, that whoever believes in Him shall not perish, but have eternal life."   John 3:16

Have you asked Jesus to come into your heart and forgive all your sins?

Have you told someone else how they can receive Jesus Christ as their Savior?

CHAPTER EIGHT

Communion of Commitment

by Jill

November 18, 1979

I'm so happy to be home today. We came last night, and our family was all together for the first time in one month! It was so good to see Jon. With a big smile, he leaped into our arms as we hugged and kissed one another. He keeps calling us "Grandma" and "Grandpa." A Japanese lady flew back with him from Kansas City, for which we were thankful. They said Jon wasn't afraid at all to go with her.

November 22, 1979

Weary! I wish we didn't have to go back for the second part of Team Training. The first session was designed for the leadership group. The second session is designed for the entire group of team members. Staying home and preparing for Christmas appeals to me.

Our neighbor, Ben, accepted Christ as his Savior! In fact, he said he "made the commitment". He waited and asked Barbara if she'd like to receive Christ's gift of salvation with him. To his surprise, he learned she already had. He was taking the initiative. She said she hadn't told him because she didn't want him to feel any pressure.

My morning was spent packing while laundering and ironing necessary items. Preparation for team training's second session was in full swing. Pulling together Jon's toys, table games, and a sack supper for latecomers while dodging neighborly company has been a challenge. The boys helped me load the car, and Jon and I sped off to the mission. He was going to stay with us this time for team training in Warwick, NY. Tod and Scot would stay with the Kenworthys, friends from the mission.

November 24, 1979

I've been in a stew today—on an emotional roller coaster. This is the first day that the entire Christ's Mission team has arrived.

The only reason I hang in here at all is because I believe Jesus is King of Kings: worthy of my total commitment, my life, my all. We are already victors—but still in warfare. Boy! Do I need to put my armor on!

I began reading the introductory remarks to the booklet, *Faith* by George Mueller. The first prerequisite to growing in faith is to know and believe His promises. Secondly, I am not to regard any iniquity in my heart.

My eyes stayed there. All these months I clung to my rights and justifiable feelings. Hurts had not always been responded to with God's love, but rather my spirit had become unloving, unforgiving. I knew right there I had to confess and see how God would direct. Peace came that I had not had for quite a while. Now I could face people with a clean heart.

A highlight for Dennis was his meeting with Mission Budget Committee in Dallas. A heavy weight was lifted off his shoulders when they said, "You don't have to make this project work. We don't expect you to feel responsible to see it happen. If it doesn't go, we will take it as from the Lord and not feel we have wasted His money, but simply obeyed."

At the conclusion of the meeting, he prayed how he would miss their fellowship, but he was unable to finish due to the strong emotions welling up inside of him.

November 29, 1979

This morning we called Tod and Scot. After talking a while, I mentioned that tomorrow would be Kenworthy's last day with them. Tod said he sure would miss them. To me, that's a miracle only God could do!

They have stayed with many people, but are always very ready for Mom and Dad to return. He said he would write them from Rome.

Tonight was the first time I have ever heard Jon really pray from his heart. He asked me to pray first which is rare. I did. He began, "Thank you, Jesus; thank you, God, that I can play hockey, and that I can build a church (with his blocks). Thank you for my daddy who works so hard. Give him strength so he can have power...."

December 9, 1979

Tod's eleventh birthday celebration began yesterday early in the morning.

He and Scot had joined us for the last weekend of training. I granted Tod permission to join us for a communion service closing team training. Scot wanted to come also. Because it is Tod's birthday, he needs some extra privileges occasionally being the oldest. I felt the midnight hour should find Scot and Jon in bed.

Tod found himself in a dimly lit room seated in a circle. Each team member took a pipe cleaner and shaped it to symbolize what he had learned the past couple weeks. Each one would place it in the center of the room making a statement of commitment to the other members of the team. I wondered if this was too heavy for Tod to handle.

My tears kept being brushed away as he watched. The communion was served voluntarily by each team member to another. I wanted to serve Tod communion on his birthday—making him feel an important part of the group. Maybe Dennis was thinking the same thing. I will wait a moment and see.

Yes, Dennis got up and headed toward our son, spoke aloud the meaning of the element and served him. A beautiful sight! A tearful one for me.

A few people later, Tod dutifully got up, lifted the communion tray and chalice and moved in my direction. He was going to serve me! Tod walked quietly in my direction and stopped—just to the left of me. My young eleven-year-old would serve the oldest member of the team, Grandma Bell. I couldn't be happier! Tears were streaming now! How proud I was, God. Thank you.

Later he told me when he looked at her humble, happy face, he didn't want her to feel left out if no one served her communion.

As it turned out, being the thirty-one-year-old blonde mother beside her, I was the last to be served. Communion with the Father had already taken place!

Tod was lying in bed. I sat by his side sensing he wanted to say something. Breaking the silence, I offered an embarrassed, "It was kind of long, wasn't it?" "Yea, but I wouldn't have missed it for anything in the world."

REFLECTIONS ON COMMITMENT

The Lord Jesus brings newness of life as He cleanses hearts and adopts us as His children for eternity, allowing us to introduce others into His kingdom.

What does the taking of communion represent?

"While they were eating, Jesus took some bread, and after a blessing, He broke it and gave it to the disciples, and said, 'Take, eat; this is My body.' And when he had taken a cup and given thanks, He gave it to them, saying, 'Drink from it, all of you; for this is My blood of the covenant, which is poured out for many for forgiveness of sins." Matthew 26:26-28

Why is it important?

"And when he had taken some bread and given thanks, He broke it and gave it to them, saying, 'This is My body which is given for you; do this in remembrance of me.' " Luke 22:19

Was this a difficult sacrifice for Jesus, the Son of God, to make?

"...Father, if You are willing, remove this cup from Me; yet not My will, but Yours be done." Luke 22:42

Is it necessary for God's children to make sacrifices at times?

Can you name a time or situation where God called you to sacrifice?

Reflecting on Christ's response, what should our attitude be?

Is God trustworthy, even with our children?

> *"...'Truly I say to you, there is no one who has left house or wife or brothers or parents or children, for the sake of the kingdom of God, who will not receive many times as much as this time and in the age to come, eternal life.' "*
>
> Luke 18:29

CHAPTER NINE

Ready to Go

by Jill

<u>February 4, 1980</u>

Ever since team training, my mood has been somewhat despondent—certainly not joyful. Resigned to what must be done, my father put it aptly, "Jill, you are like the little girl I remember standing defiantly in her crib, clutching the rail and clenching her teeth." That is how I feel. The fall season brought Dennis and me to Warwick, New Jersey, for some weeks of team training. The first several weeks were required for team leaders, during which my husband was chosen to be Project Director for Italy Project I. Being with the other leaders was crucial for building relationships that could withstand the many struggles and defeats we would face. The last night ended our growing time together with a commitment service. Each one had to pronounce his/her commitment to the team project always expecting the best to come about and accepting each other with their faults and strengths until the end of the project. The commitments were strong and intense and certainly could not be made flippantly. However, a beautiful feeling of release and rightness clamored for notoriety when the evening had finished and each one had stated his/her oath of commitment.

<u>February 6, 1980</u>

Barbara came running over partly hysterical, balancing the cupcakes in one hand and green frosting and red coconut in the other. Red coconut spattered on the green entry rug. Throwing the items on the counter, she sputtered her request for me to frost the cupcakes and deliver them to Douglas' kindergarten class. Tears continued to fall. She relayed the past few hours events of taking him to the hospital and learning he may have leukemia. Crying, we prayed for God's grace and deliverance. Dennis drove her to the hospital. We were concerned to see what strength she would find in her new-found faith to meet this ugly hour.

The next day she told me she had sat with her Bible open most of the night reading and watching an especially bright star God had positioned over Douglas' bed. He knew. He cared.

She prayed. "God, if you take Douglas, I will still love you, but I won't understand. God, I am not trying to be fresh, but if you do take him, you are not going to have time to listen to anyone else's prayers. He is so rambunctious. You will have to spend all your time looking after him. He will turn heaven upside down. God, I am not going to make you any promises because I probably couldn't keep them. I am just human—just me."

February 20, 1980

Today the news came—an apartment has been found for us in Florence, Italy. God *is* at work. Rather strange contemplating the idea of moving back into an apartment again. Imagine! A person I have never met chooses an apartment for me in a city and country I have never even visited yet. Encouraging it is, though, after hearing of a man who has been looking for an apartment in Florence for seven months without success.

February 26, 1980
     Yesterday Dennis stayed home as we began the first plans for packing. We went over lists of needed items to purchase. Sometimes it is difficult to keep good attitudes toward each other when there are normal tensions of money, leaving and differing opinions.

     I made myself get up and be in God's Word this morning, because that is the way I survive. Keep a Christ-like attitude. I have been disappointed in my own concern of seeing the list of "needs" become reality now. I don't want to be so attached to material things—but rather recognize God will provide what we need. He has provided faithfully the past year. But still, I begin to feel like we won't have enough money to meet our needs.

     Last week we started studying *Your Life in Christ* with Ben and Barbara. Our time together was good. Two things stood out. Once again, the Spirit is at work in Ben. He shared how on his last trip in his hotel room he turned on cable TV to watch a movie. A prostitute was teaching her daughter how to become one. It sickened him. He turned it off and picked up the Gideon Bible reading it for a good while. Very different for him, he said! When he returned home, he canceled his cable TV as it is not needed for the Christian walk.

     Ben doesn't get excited too quickly about things. Mild-mannered, tailored gray suits attire him. Dennis and I were saying we didn't know if God would bring about any believers in Rome or not. We were dwelling on our lack of ability rather than God's ABILITY.

     Ben jumped out of his seat landing halfway across the table and shouted, "Hundreds! I know God is going to give you hundreds!"

He doesn't know how encouraging his faith and affirmation were. Our desire is for God to provide fellowship and continued growth in His Word with other believers.

We had completed our time at the church mission house to help us prepare for our service in Italy. We had made many friends and had shared some special family times of travel, skiing and hosting a special Christmas gathering for grandparents, aunts and uncles.

Time had passed, making it necessary for another round of packing duty. Everything had to be enumerated on a special list and packed in a careful manner for a long, rough trip by ship. Packing seemed to be unending day after day. One set of boxes had to be packed for our six-month stay in Florence and the remainder was for setting up housekeeping in Rome. Shopping for just the right necessities, enough suitcases and some clothes for the boys to grow into filled the days as well. Many lists were demanding my attention as well as coping with shadows of lonely feelings as we prepared to leave our precious family counterparts and our country. My parents came the last week to help us box up all the big items and to see the packing finished. They had been a source of encouragement to us throughout many months desiring only the Father's will and direction for our lives. No, it had not been easy to accept initially. Dad had often preached the necessity of giving one's life to Christ and being willing to serve Him in another country, telling them of Christ's good news of salvation. Many young people from his various churches throughout the years had indeed ministered for the Lord in other countries. Years before, he had been convinced that the decision to be a missionary in another country would be a privilege for any followers of Christ—until his only daughter and her family had been directed to move so far away. His and mother's muscles of spiritual maturity were stretched as they were called upon to accept and apply what they had taught and preached for years. They prayed for us regularly, desiring God's best for us. If this was His direction for us, they were pleased to help and encourage us.

These same feelings were shared by my husband's mother, who also came the last few day before we left the States. She offered her gracious love and support in many ways and always has been a great prayer warrior for us.

March 14, 1980

Barbara and Ben will store our boxes for three months and then have Abarim Freight Company pick them up and ship them to Rome.

God has been faithfully giving me little gifts—extra special acts of love from friends: a letter, a book, a hymnal, a set of notes on a writing class, $25.

A special treat one day was having my husband turn off the typewriter, sit me down in the kitchen and serve me a cup of tea with German chocolate cake.

Another of God's caring gifts is that the team will be renting a villa to use as their headquarters. There will be adequate office space and a yard. I can hardly wait to see it.

REFLECTIONS ON GOD'S LOVE

Small acts of kindness and big responses to needs communicate God's interactive love.

What precludes our commitment to working closely together with God's family?

> *"You shall love the Lord your God with all your heart and with all your soul and with all your might."*
>
> Deuteronomy 6:5

How is this truth on display in your life? How will it look in the lives of others?

> *"So then we pursue the things which make for peace and the building up of one another."*   Romans 14:19

What is the long-range perspective of good coming from a suffocating trial, such as a child's illness?

> *"Therefore, having been justified by faith, we have peace with God through our Lord Jesus Christ, through whom also we have obtained our introduction by faith into this grace in which we stand; and we exult in hope of the glory of God. And not only this, but we also exult in our tribulations, knowing that tribulation brings about perseverance; and perseverance, proven character; and proven character, hope; and hope does not disappoint, because the love of God has been poured out within our hearts through the Holy Spirit who was given to us."*
>
> Romans 5:1-5

Keeping a proper attitude towards our mate during a time of tension in our lives is a challenge. Using 1 Corinthians 13:1-8, identify the principles of love that you may need to be reminded of.

"If I speak with the tongues of men and of angels, but do not have love, I have become a noisy gong or a clanging cymbal. If I have the gift of prophecy, and know all mysteries and all knowledge; and if I have all faith, so as to remove mountains, but do not have love, I am nothing. And if I give all my possessions to feed the poor, and if I surrender my body to be burned, but do not have love, it profits me nothing.

"Love is patient, love is kind and is not jealous; love does not brag and is not arrogant, does not act unbecomingly; it does not seek its own, is not provoked, does not take into account a wrong suffered, does not rejoice in unrighteousness, but rejoices with the truth; bears all things, believes all things, hopes all things, endures all things.

"Love never fails; but if there are gifts of prophecy, they will be done away; if there are tongues, they will cease; if there is knowledge, it will be done away."
I Corinthians 13: 1-8

Who does this day belong to?

"This is the day which the Lord has made; Let us rejoice and be glad in it." Psalm 118:24

Why is it good for us to read God's Word each day and talk to Him in prayer?

"Your word I have treasured in my heart, that I may not sin against You."　　　　　　　　Psalm 119:11

"The effective prayer of a righteous man can accomplish much."　　　　　　　　James 5:16b

What did Jesus teach His disciples concerning material needs?

"...For this reason I say to you, do not worry about your life, as to what you will eat; nor for your body, as to what you will put on...Consider the ravens, for they neither sow nor reap; they have no storeroom nor barn, and yet God feeds them; how much more valuable you are than the birds!...Consider the lilies, how they grow: they neither toil nor spin; but I tell you, not even Solomon in all his glory clothed himself like one of these. But if God so clothes the grass in the field, which is alive today and tomorrow is thrown into the furnace, how much more will He clothe you? You men of little faith!"
Luke 12:22,24,27,28

What promise determines our ability to give our children to the Lord God to serve Him in full-time ministry?

" . . .from childhood you have known the sacred writings which are able to give you the wisdom that leads to salvation through faith which is in Christ Jesus...so that the man of God may be adequate, equipped for every good work."　　　　　　　　II Timothy 3:15,17

CHAPTER TEN

Welcome to Italy

by Jill and Dennis

The day to depart finally arrived. All team members met at the JFK airport in New Jersey in a rather small private room with the mission director and others from the mission. Various family members and friends joined in to say their good-byes and bid their good wishes. Cameras rapidly flashed pictures.

Our helper friend, Jenny, met us at the airport. She was to live with us in Florence and care for our youngest son, Jon, while we would be in language school for six months. Jenny was another one of our Father's special answers to prayer. Childcare during our transition period to a new culture concerned us. Jenny's coming had been another one of the Lord's exclamation marks behind his word "Go!" She had come to know the Lord Jesus as her Savior in her high school years while attending the youth group at church. We were thankful for her willing spirit to help. Now, however, I was wondering if she was experiencing the same writhing pains of homesickness that I was.

I had gone downstairs to a special phone area to telephone my parents and hear their precious voices for the last time for a good while. Restraining tears and controlling sobs was not possible. I was dreading boarding that plane! I did not want to go. My heart was sick with painful throbs of homesickness—and we had not even left yet. Of course, the public could only see silent teardrops. My children had my deepest sympathy, understanding and encouragement. We would all love and help each other. I felt sorry for my husband if he were feeling as nauseous as I was and suddenly being the leader of 30 homesick people. He seemed calm and in control. After a good prayer time and more pictures, we said our good-byes and boarded the plane. My husband had situated the older boys, and I sat beside our youngest in the middle group section of seats. I felt so tired and wished I could disappear. I was to don a smiling face and cheerfully encourage the other gals and fellows who were leaving as well. Lord, help me. *"Be strong and courageous. Do not tremble or be dismayed for the Lord your God is with you wherever you go."* Joshua 1:9. Thank you, Lord. I sat rather quietly, not seeking great amounts of conversation and hoping the time would pass quickly. Meanwhile, the boys were fine and had fallen asleep after the good evening meal. I could not relax my systems enough to sleep, even though I felt so tired. I sat quietly.

After fourteen hours of flying, our plane was arriving in Rome, Italy. This would certainly be novel—a new country, new ways, new language. I would watch it all unfold. We got off the plane outside the terminal and had to walk up to the building. Standing in long lines thereafter to have all passports and papers acknowledged was the next step. Finally, we were able to get all of our luggage and wheel it over to a special counter for customs. What would they do? Look in every suitcase, every trunk and not allow us to have all that we brought?

Outside the terminal all of our items were being loaded on a large bus which promptly transported us to our place of rest for several days—the Villa Betania, a Baptist Hospitality House. Driving into Rome held our attention as we carefully observed the landscapes and structures of our new culture. Yes, it did seem older and dirtier. We wound our way through small side streets and approached the big friendly mission house. This very large villa was immaculately clean. Immediately, one began to notice various differences. In crossing the seas, we had exchanged soft, plush carpet for hard, cold marble floors. We were able to situate our family in two adjoining rooms and a private bath, which added to our comfort.

The first night's sleep for me was interrupted with nightmares and crying. I was churning inside and hungry, as well. I woke my husband and within a few minutes, the children were awake and hungry also. We were all suffering from a dramatic lifestyle change—coupled with jetlag. Our bodies were not ignoring their habitual schedules. I had included snacks in our packing. Eating familiar snacks with some delicious Italian fresh fruit, we all satisfied our tummy's hunger pangs and went back to sleep.

During our next couple days, Jon was not feeling well. I stayed with him, while everyone else left to sightsee and get a feel for this new land. My days seemed long and stifled in the cold cement rooms while waiting to hear everyone's exciting new discoveries of the day. We were enjoying some new pasta dishes at suppertime that one of our dear leaders willingly prepared. He had served in Italy before and had already begun to develop his skill with Italian cuisine.

A couple of days later, in the month of April, 1980, we again loaded another bus with all the team's luggage and began to travel to Florence, north of Rome. Jon was now feeling much better and so was I, being able to get out and actually see more of our new territorial surroundings.

Miles of natural beauty formed the panorama from our moving vehicle, seeming as though we were actually viewing scenes from postcards. Small medieval towns punctuated the mountains. Conversation among the team members bounced vigorously. Each was trying to picture their new temporary homes. The anticipation was almost more than one could handle calmly in the three-hour drive from Rome to Florence. I was sure we would be living in a tattered, dirty hole in the wall with broken-down furniture. Obviously, I did not know Italians very well!

Finally, we arrived in the Florentine city itself. The first stop would be the Eenigenburg's "new" apartment. Anxiety crept in. "Lord, what are we going to drive up to? How should I react with so many other people to watch me? I need to act as though I like it, right? Oh, Lord, they must be feeling scared, too. What if the children do not like it? I need time alone with them, not with an audience, to view our family right now. Help me, Father."

The bus pulled up alongside a massive gray cement building. An announcement was made that this is where Dennis and Jill's family would live. A small cement world without much greenery is what it seemed to be. No yards. An occasional tree helped give life to the cool grayness. Our family and a few others excitedly apprehended the key from the doorman and ascended the stairs to our front door—which opened into an attractive entryway, clean and neat. Continuing to stand there, I gazed to my right. I was utterly amazed to see the elegance of this furnished apartment. The enormous chandelier over the lovely cherry wood dining room table captured my attention. The apartment was clean with handsome furniture arranged in an attractive manner. The boys' room was colorfully decorated in red and blue plaid. Even the master bedroom had a king-size bed beautifully made up! The kitchen was quite small, but contained most of the utensils necessary for cooking. The dishes for use in the dining room were lovely china. Our meals would be eaten there because the kitchen lacked space for table and chairs. Also, there was a clothes washer, which was a great surprise. Most of the rooms had little terraces where one could enjoy fresh air, even though streets were trafficked heavily with buses, cars, trucks, mopeds and cycles. Thank you, Father, for taking care of us.

Our team family members had been very considerate to wait outside a good while, allowing us a bit of time to see our new home first. One by one they came in to see the apartment, trying to imagine where each of them might live. Language school had arranged for each team member to live with Italian families to help promote quicker language comprehension and communication. They were braver than I.

After the bus pulled away to deliver each team member to their new home, we were able to get more familiar with our new home. As suppertime approached, our only decision could be to go out to a restaurant for supper, as we had no food yet. We had no car either, and we did not know the location of a good restaurant close by. We began walking, certain that we would come upon a place of eating tucked into the combined residential and business area. We walked and walked—long block after long block. No restaurant. We had become aware of the fact that we were not going to find a place. Hunger was becoming pronounced. We decided to go back to the little store by our apartment and try to order food for sandwiches to take home. Successfully, we managed to get some ham, freshly baked bread and accompaniments, as well as cereal and milk for breakfast. Wearily, we plodded home to set forth our first meal. To our sullen surprise, a couple of doors down from the little store was a small restaurant filled to capacity. Happily, we decided that tomorrow after church, we would dine there. A bit of enthusiasm sparked our steps now.

Sunday was our first full day at our new home. Yes, our plan was to meet the team members that morning at the Chiesa Evangelica church in Florence. It was associated with Brethren Assembly—as would be the church we would be starting in Rome.

We took the city bus to arrive at church and meandered through the narrow brick streets to the correct building. Entering the auditorium and seeing other team members offered a bit of opportunity to learn of the various living situations with their new Italian families. A worshipful atmosphere was pleasant to behold, as Scripture was read and hymns were sung. The oral language was not yet understood, but the emotional language began to state clearly that we were all part of one family, Jesus Christ being our Savior.

Contentedly, we took the public bus back home, knowing where we would go immediately for a good meal. Confidently, we walked over to the restaurant—only to learn that reservations must be made for Sunday. All the tables were booked. We would not have even known how to ask for a reservation. We settled for another meal of ham sandwiches at home.

The very next morning, we began language school. When classes were over, we registered our two oldest boys at the American School of Florence and later managed to put away the remainder of our packed items.

Jenny and I began to learn our way to the grocery store. We took the bus twice a week to the supermarket and carried all the plastic bags home via the bus. Effort and balance were required to keep the bags from spilling over into the aisles while we were jerked to and fro from the movements of the bus. Each Sunday afternoon, the team would come to our home for light refreshments and a time of Bible study, sharing and prayer. Our home provided a central locale for team functions.

May 15, 1980

I have needed to take my eyes off what being a hostess has meant in the past. Always organized, invited and planned have had to become flexible qualities that focus on making the guests feel at home and welcomed. My attention needs to be focused on them, not the surrounding paraphernalia.

When I feel inconvenienced to welcome another "intruder," I need to resist the urge to withdraw or ignore them as I have done in the past when it seemed overwhelming. Rather, response to that temptation should be replaced by looking up, giving a warm smile and greeting—also learning to let them help as they desire. Things don't always have to be done my way. The important thing is that jobs get done and all feel accepted and cared for.

My more relaxed spirit changes the mood of our home full of people. Some go back with the children and read or play games, others come in the kitchen and are cleaning up with no assistance from me while others are visiting or enjoying magazines sent from the States.

Looking at inconveniences as opportunities to worship, my hospitality becomes a service of worship in loving my brothers and sisters in Christ, reflecting His nature. I am understanding more of what was meant when He said, *"Who are My brothers? Who are My sisters? My brothers and sisters are those who do the will of My Father."* To treat brothers and sisters in Christ as I would my own family is, I believe, what He is saying.

May 13, 1980
Adjusting to a new culture has proven to be "real" work. It is like having to use muscles that you didn't have to use at home—leg muscles walking to school, arm muscles carrying groceries on the bus, mental muscles seeking to understand Italian, and linguistic muscles attempting new sounds. The imbalance and insecurity experienced are often referred to as "culture shock." Two responses that Jill and I discovered are fatigue and hunger. Every evening I feel like I have just completed a camping hike with the local Boy Scout troop. My sons, Tod 11, Scot 9, and Jon 4, have at least shown evidence of the "hunger syndrome." "Leftovers" have become an obsolete word in our domestic vocabulary.

The challenge of language school and a new culture has been intensified by other responsibilities. Each of the project leaders (5) has team-related and organizational duties besides the 25 hours per week in the classroom. We have been blessed with a very mature group of two and one-half year team members (18). In order to grow in our unity, we meet weekly for inductive Bible study and then once a week for prayer in small groups.

As we study Philippians, we find that Paul's joy is related to the *"greater progress of the Gospel"*, not his personal sufferings. I desire to share Paul's attitude instead of being discouraged about my poor use of the Italian language or frustrating inconveniences.

REFLECTIONS ON SACRIFICE

Self's ugly head rises up to distract us from opportunities to reflect Christ's character.

Our courage and strength comes from the Lord in desperate times. What invitation does He give us?

"Come to Me, all who are weary and heavy laden, and I will give you rest." Matthew 11:28

If we let Him carry our burdens, how heavy is our load?

"Take my yoke upon you and learn from Me, for I am gentle and humble in heart, and you will find rest for your souls. For My yoke is easy and My burden is light." Matthew 11:29,30

What can we learn from Him?

How can you apply it?

Do you believe the Lord is with you wherever you go?

> *"Have I not commanded you? Be strong and coura-*
> *geous! Do not tremble or be dismayed, for the Lord*
> *you God is with you wherever you go."* Joshua 1:9

How have you sensed His presence today?

Is it good for us to make sacrifices for our Lord God?
Who is our model?

What type of sacrifice needs to surround our inconveniences?

> *"Through Him then, let us continually offer up a sacri-*
> *fice of praise to God, that is, the fruit of lips that give*
> *thanks to His name. And do not neglect doing good and*
> *sharing, for with such sacrifices God is pleased."*
> Hebrews 13:15,16

Can we out-give the Lord?

> *"Give, and it will be given to you. They will pour into*
> *your lap a good measure—pressed down, shaken*
> *together, and running over. For by your standard of*
> *measure it will be measured to you in return."*
> Luke 6:38

As we obey and imitate Christ in the challenging events of
life, how is it an act of worship?

> *"For though we walk in the flesh, we do not war ac-*
> *cording to the flesh . . . we are taking every thought*
> *captive to the obedience of Christ..."*
> II Corinthians 10:3,5b

Are you referred to as Christ's brother or sister when He says,

> *"Who is My mother and who are My brothers?...For whoever shall do the will of My Father who is in heaven, he is My brother and sister and mother."*

Matthew 12:48b,50

CHAPTER ELEVEN

Aggravating
Adjustments

by Jill

August 18, 1980

I haven't recorded my thoughts for a long time. Much has happened and is happening to me—good and bad. Sometime I will elaborate more fully. But now I just want to say again, God is good. God is faithful. God is all-powerful. God knows me, and I know Him because of the loss He suffered in sending His Son—because of the sufferings His Son Jesus endured, leaving His lovely home with His Father and sacrificing Himself for an ungrateful people, an ungrateful world and, often, an ungrateful me.

While being here over the months, I have lost perspective, lost my goals, sometimes feeling I have lost my identity as well. Home has loomed larger, more important in my mind, family more precious. Inconveniences have preyed upon my mind ready to kill the tender shoots of acceptance. A need to feast at Jesus' feet has been thwarted, even small snacks dismissed as the urgent clouded out the important. Thus, my mind has become pallid and limp with aching, having blurred capacity to function. I have felt low to the ground, body bent in anguish.

God sent a friend who didn't especially want to make another trip, but brought her van down from Germany for our sakes to help complete its registration for immediate use. Shirley Rodgers has been a missionary in the jungle bush of Mexico with her four children. She knows the hurts and the pain, but God has gifted her with a good sense of adventure and humor, both of which I often lack. She reminded me of a lesson I had forcefully "learned" earlier.

Say, "Thank You." So simple. So important.

I know You are making me into the woman You want to use more completely for Your purposes. Thank You.

Thank You for the freezer door that always falls off. Thank You for the marble floors I find difficult to clean. Thank You for the overwhelming abundance of company that seems to require every spare minute. Thank You for the young lady You provided to do all my regular tasks at home and for the way she does them! Thank You for the inadequacies my husband feels and for the difficulties my children face like having free summer days while we are in language school. Each one You are molding into precious men of God. Thank You.

We are a rarity: my husband and I and our family. We love with a firm commitment. Students from all over the world see this kind of commitment as impossible and, therefore, unobtainable and unrealistic. Their pictures of families are much less defined with less commitment in their human relationships. I feel like light in a dark society. We are all they taste, often all they see of the infinite God. A taste, a glimpse. Stability, solidarity, but many will turn away, *"...through whom we have received grace and apostleship to bring about the obedience of faith among all Gentiles...."* Romans 1:5

August 20, 1980

Friday we had a substitute teacher the last hour. She, of course, was determined to teach properly and corrected every wrong syllable spoken. The class began to give her fits playing very dumb. So she went around asking each person why they were studying Italian.

"I am studying because of my husband's work," I responded.

She asked if it was commercial. Telling her no, I explained that we were with a group here to plant a church in Rome. Intrigued, she pulled her chair up closer and the rest of the hour was centered on me—a wide-open opportunity to share the Gospel in my stumbling Italian before the class.

She said, "But there are many churches here in Rome? Why would you want to start another?"

I remember clearly my first statement. "La gente hanno abastanza delle chiese." (The people have enough churches). From there I can't recall exactly what I said. I was so excited, nervous and trying desperately to get across the importance of knowing Jesus personally!

The whole class seemed supportive of me, helping translate, if necessary, and listening intently. The teacher said she had never met a pastor's wife before and asked about what my role involved. She seemed spellbound and never corrected me once! She was the first Italian with whom I could share the gospel.

After class, she left without saying a word. I don't know what she thought, but the Spirit had a lot of work to do enlightening her through my Italian!

1979 Honda with Texas license plates

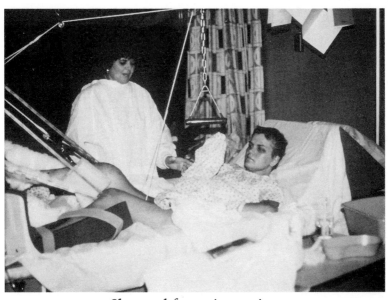

Shattered femur in traction.
Jill's mom visiting at San Camillo Hospital.

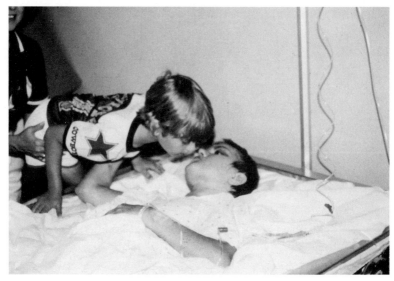

Son Jon is eager to give her a kiss.

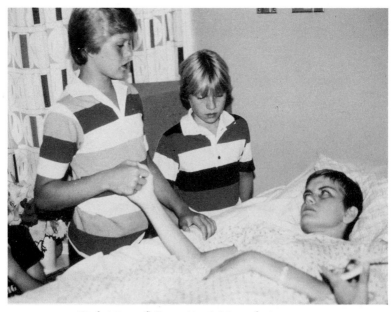

Tod 13 and Scot 11 visiting their mom.

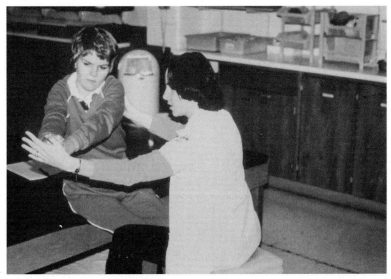

Occupational therapy

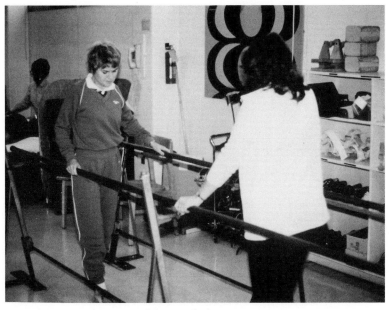

Physical therapy

Picnicking in wheelchair with Dennis and parents in Kansas City.

Dennis and Jill celebrating Valentine's Day again!

August 25, 1980

Our oldest son had some great insights. From all the art pieces and museums he has seen, his comment was, "They always picture Christ as powerless, either as a baby or dead, hanging on the cross. If I ever had an opportunity to paint a picture, I would put Christ on the throne, and Mary and Joseph bowing down to Him."

The summer months were drawing to a close. We needed to go to Rome and register the boys at the American Overseas School of Rome and make contact with someone they could stay with to begin school. Language school for us would not finish until the end of September. The Lord provided a fine missionary family who were glad to host the boys for a couple of weeks. They also had a son who was Tod's age. Willingly, they took in our oldest two boys to help them begin school on time.

September 13, 1980

My heart has been heavy having left the boys in Rome to start school. I know what they are facing. Every day is the most difficult task they have ever been asked to do. It showed on their faces when they returned from school the first day.

They are in a lovely home with lovely people, but that long bus ride to school is a real endurance contest. Transferring on three rickety city buses takes one hour and fifteen minutes one way to school. Usually there is no place to sit. I wish we could afford school bus service for them. At least they would have a seat and could be with friends. We will have to see how they manage. Scot has trouble finding anything low enough to hold onto for balance.

Our old familiar pastime of packing became necessary once again for our move to Rome.

Gladly, we finished language school and were anxious to be a complete family again. The time had come for our dear friend Jenny to return to the States. She had been a big help in many ways. We would miss her.

REFLECTIONS ON SUFFERING

Sharing in Christ's sufferings is a deplorable task apart from the grace He gently gives with eternal results.

What are some ways Christ suffered and what was His response?

> *"...while being reviled, He did not revile in return; while suffering, He uttered no threats, but kept entrusting Himself to Him who judges righteously..."*
>   I Peter 2:23

Why was He willing to suffer?

> *"...He Himself bore our sins in His body on the cross, so that we might die to sin and live to righteousness; for by His wounds you were healed."*   I Peter 2:24

Should we expect to share in His sufferings?

> *"For you have been called for this purpose, since Christ also suffered for you, leaving you an example for you to follow in His steps…"* I Peter 2:21

Regardless of responsibilities and expectations we put on ourselves, what priority does Jesus encourage Martha to make?

> *"Now as they were traveling along, He entered a village; and a woman named Martha welcomed Him into her home. She had a sister called Mary, who was seated at the Lord's feet, listening to His word. But Martha was distracted with all her preparations; and she came up to Him and said, 'Lord, do You not care that my sister has left me to do all the serving alone? Then tell her to help me.' But the Lord answered and said to her, 'Martha, Martha, you are worried and bothered about so many things; but only one thing is necessary, for Mary has chosen the good part, which shall not be taken away from her."* Luke 10:38-42

Why had Mary chosen the better use of time?

What is significant about listening to Jesus?

Can you schedule regular appointments with the Lord Jesus? His schedule is flexible.

What are we to be thankful for?

> *"…in everything give thanks; for this is God's will for you in Christ Jesus."* I Thess. 5:18

Can you give thanks for all things today? Who changes the heart focus?

Who is the light of the world? Can we have that light?

> *"Then Jesus again spoke to them, saying, 'I am the Light of the world; he who follows Me will not walk in the darkness, but will have the Light of life."*   John 8:12

CHAPTER TWELVE

Rome Becomes Home

by Jill

The orange van we had acquired was packed and ready to transport our things to Rome. Finally, I would get to see our next place of residence. What would it be like?

We drove up to a nicely kept neighborhood where the apartment complex was located. Getting out of the car, we rounded the corner where the brick wall separated the apartment dwellers from the passersby. Unlocking the iron gate, we walked through the nicely landscaped walkway to our apartment building. Using another key, we entered and took the elevator to the third floor where the marble floor would lead us around the corner to our front door. Sunshine freely entered the large glass windows exposing a lovely apartment with great possibilities for a cheery home. Yes, the walls needed a good painting and the rooms needed a good cleaning. But we were pleased and thankful.

No, there would not be hot water or electricity until arrangements could be made with the companies. The boys could study in the evenings at Villa Clara where the team was living, and we could shower there, too. A couple of team members had put some cots and a divan in the apartment for us, so we did have a place to rest our tired bodies.

I remember well our first night in Rome. We had gotten all of the boys to bed in our large dining-living room area where the cots were. With no lights to read our mail by,

Dennis and I huddled together on the floor backed up to a small dividing wall with candles lit. We began to read a variety of precious letters from dear friends in the States. Some had substantial checks in them to help supply our needs and desires. Tears came to our eyes. We felt so alone and forlorn with everything so new. The Lord knew that we needed these gifts of love that particular night. We smiled. We thanked Him.

One can survive without certain conveniences which we take for granted and expect to be available at all times. Living without electricity or hot water was challenging, though not impossible. It did test our endurance for three weeks. The night air would cool our milk and juice for breakfast. Doing laundry by hand required muscle, but accomplished a necessary task. A special birthday gift to me that particular year was electricity; it was turned on the very day of my birthday. I found real joy in being able to push the light switch and actually see the room brighten. The first week we all prized electricity as a valuable commodity and used the lights rather sparingly. It was also necessary not to overload the electrical circuits and burn out fuses, which happened all too easily. Wise usage of electricity was a new important lesson.

We began to research the best buys available needed to set up housekeeping. We bought a good refrigerator, a gas stove, a small kitchen table and chairs. Second-hand, we purchased kitchen cabinets, a rebuilt washing machine and a lovely marble dining room set. Our "set-up" funds allowed this. However, boxes had replaced the boy's bed frames and exposed poles held our clothes rather than closet-like armoires. Suitcases took the place of dresser drawers. A few folding chairs were added to the old black and white vinyl couch in the living room for adequate seating. Any resemblance to home's coziness was lost. The cold marble floors needed rugs and the bare windows needed curtains. We still did not have light fixtures, but settled happily for inserting light bulbs that we could now turn on. Life could resume its somewhat normal posture.

With the children in school each day and Dennis at the office, I began to feel that I was stowed away in a cold, marble prison. Lacking warm, cheery spots or nicely decorated rooms to please one's visionary senses, caused me to ask," Lord, is this where you are wanting me to be? I feel like a prisoner. Do you care about my needs? Please, Lord, provide for our family's new home so that even the boys won't feel embarrassed to have in their friends. Lord, we're desiring to get to know our neighbors and to host them. We want them to see that You care for Your children."

As cold weather advanced, heat was permitted 12 hours a day from November through March. Physically, I became quite ill with colds and sinus problems. It was taking a while for my body to adjust to the cooler living conditions. Thankfully our electric blanket kept me warm during these days of illness and depression. Tears seemed to be my constant companion.

January 14, 1981
Dear Mom and Dad,

I've hit rock bottom—really questioning if God in fact, really cares for me. How could He let me suffer like this? My own dad wouldn't make me, and he'd do all he could to provide; so why doesn't God? Anyway, once you feel God isn't a loving God and doesn't love you, it wipes out your motivation for everything. Why endure?

I had spells of uncontrollable crying. Sunday afternoon Dennis, while he washed the dishes, began helping me gain perspective. My mind was so numb. I couldn't process one more thing. I got a pencil and wrote down all the wise counsel he gave me to read and re-read when my mind was in a healthier state. As he talked and prayed for me, I felt at least alive and went with him and the boys to the team meeting to benefit from being with them.

Also, I'd begun reading Edith Schaeffer's *Affliction*. It helped me with perspective on suffering, and I want to learn more. God didn't intend it to be this way originally, but the rebelliousness of Satan commenced it. God chose a very difficult but singular solution in sending His Son. Otherwise, without His suffering, our only alternative would be self-destruction under Satan. How horrible! God sees the overall picture of history from past to present, the overall plan. We're participating in a small segment of it right now.

Someone said Satan tests us in our weak areas, but God tests us in our strengths. I surely see this here—and that's how He makes us stronger in them, and we become more refined instruments, stronger tools for greater tasks. "Tremendous victories come from tremendous battles,"Edith Schaeffer states.

Also for me the question was, how do I interpret God's love for me? Is it dependent on circumstances or material blessing? He is not Santa Claus. When my desires or contentment is based on either of these two things, my happiness is not being found in God—and that's what He desires. I felt I'd grown tremendously in those two areas only to wake up to a heart full of bitterness and resentment. This lesson all over again? Yuck!

God is making me more dependent on Him alone. He doesn't want my happiness to center on circumstances or things! Well, I'm praising Him for drawing me out of the gloom and strengthening me.

Healing began to come to my spirit as I began to apply our Lord's words from His Holy Scriptures. I knew that the Lord had brought us here and that I should be thankful for a nice place to live. My focus needed to shift from past cultural norms to the present cultural norms, even if it meant wearing a head scarf to bed to keep my scalp warm. I determined to get well, to wear more clothing for warmth and to begin looking for ministry opportunities.

February 9, 1981

Yesterday, Sunday, I went with the team and began approaching "specially selected" individuals with the Good News of Jesus Christ. Dressed finely in my new Howard Wolf suit God had graciously supplied, I would meet the women in their elegant furs with confidence. I want to make clear, however, my confidence was not in the suit, but in the Giver of the suit.

I carefully surveyed the person before going timidly up and asking if they had seen this tract or if they had received one. I enjoy finding obscure ones after the team already has disassembled and engaged in conversation. I carefully gave out two tracts without engaging in much further con-versation to one girl sitting in the small park area of the piazza and another young woman in front of the bar who was waiting for a friend. I longed to be able to get the words out of my mouth to ask what they thought about Jesus Christ. The words did not come. The fear of what happens when you open your mouth was too great. I was quiet. An older woman with blue eyebrow pencil had been sitting at a little table for quite sometime. I approached her. Finally, the words were forced out of my mouth. "What do you think of Gesu Cristo?"

She was courteous and did say she believed in Christ and this was first in importance. She didn't see the need for our group to be here because a major part of the people already believe in Christ. She said maybe the youth needed it. When I asked if she were sure where she would go when she died, she said it depends on the judgment of God. Satan has confused man with part truth and part lies in a profoundly devastating manner to the soul.

No one accepted Christ or did handstands about receiving the truth. But Christ has planted a seed of desire to be able to effectively share Him with others here in Rome. I love being out on the street and find it so challenging. It takes courage, boldness and <u>humility</u>. Such a refreshing challenge—to wiggle inside people's hearts, to see where they stand, to present the truth of their "heart condition" and to give them a prescription, which they can have filled or not.

"But godliness actually is a means of great gain, when accompanied by contentment." I Timothy 6:6

I needed great gain right now, and I certainly needed contentment with the many gifts that the Lord had already given me—a faithful husband, loving children, food to eat, clothes to wear and shelter. Focusing on the positive with thankfulness was much healthier for me and better use of my time. When Our Father would want us to host (comfortably) Italians and other friends, He would provide the items necessary. In the meantime, I needed to learn contentment with what He had already given.

May 2, 1981

God has been faithfully building me up in Him as I have been putting Him in a place of priority each day—my only way to make it! I am memorizing Ephesians 6:10-20 on the warfare and have gained a lot of insights. We need to be prepared and alert, having our weaponry ready for the enemy who is subtle and destructive. His fiery missiles can be devastating! I am happy, content in Christ today. I dare not put hope in anything else.

We can live for the things we want, we desire, we deserve—or we can live for Christ. By live, I mean putting all our mental and physical energies to use for God's glory. What are His riches? What are His promises? We can claim His promises—but we need to know what they are. I can claim peace, joy, contentment. I cannot claim a beautifully furnished home or to have my children or husband forever. He may give these things, but we must be careful in whom or what we have placed our contentment.

Relearning this lesson is not fun. I have wrestled, cried and ached to the depths of my soul. This has changed the way I pray—at least, it has made me greatly aware of how I pray and what the intent or motive is behind it.

May 8, 1981

Jon has been invited to a "Halloween-type party" at Angelo's for the Italian carnivale. The costumes the children wear are incredibly detailed in design and costly. They wear them all month. I was pleased Jon was willing to go by himself to the party. Angelo is eight, quite tall. There Jon stood in his makeshift costume: brown snow boots, faded black cowboy outfit, Tod's old cowboy hat and army rifle in hand. Opposite of the others' splendid array, he marched off to join the party. I was glad he had the courage to go. Two minutes later I heard the doorbell ring. My little cowboy was standing there, tears streaming down his cheeks and sobbing. All the others were so much bigger than he and he felt out of place. Tod, Scot and I were nearly in tears with him. I held him, comforted him. Later when we all prayed, he thanked the Lord for Angelo inviting him to the party, "but I didn't feel comfortable," he said.

REFLECTIONS ON GOD'S LOVE

Healthy people are content in their godliness.

Do you ever feel that God does not love you?

What reminders are helpful to our hurting hearts?

> *"For the Lord your God is in your midst, A victorious warrior. He will exult over you with joy, He will be quiet in His love, He will rejoice over you with shouts of joy."*   Zephaniah 3:17

From this verse, how is God personal in His love?

Is God aware of our needs?

> *"Do not worry then, saying, 'What will we eat?' or 'What will we drink?' or 'What will we wear for clothing?'*

...for your heavenly Father knows that you need all these things."   Matthew 6:31, 32b

Can He be trusted to give us good gifts?

"If you then, being evil, know how to give good gifts to your children, how much more will your Father who is in heaven give what is good to those who ask Him!"
                                        Matthew 7:11

Is God always going to give us everything we want?

"Therefore the Lord longs to be gracious to you, and therefore He waits on high to have compassion on you. For the Lord is a God of justice; how blessed are all those who long for Him." Isaiah 30:18

"And He will be the stability of your times, A wealth of salvation, wisdom and knowledge; the fear of the Lord is his treasure."   Isaiah 33:6

Is God going to provide for our needs?

"And my God will supply all your needs according to His riches in glory in Christ Jesus."   Philippians 4:19

In the midst of physical illness, what can our focus of praise be?

"...O restore me to health and let me live! Lo, for my own welfare I had great bitterness; It is You who has kept my soul from the pit of nothingness, for You have case all my sins behind Your back." Isaiah 38:16b, 17

CHAPTER THIRTEEN

Trust and Obey
by Jill

As I began to focus less on my own desires, and more on our Father's purpose for placing us in Rome, my desires began to correspond with His. The team was meeting individuals interested in studying the Bible after their street meetings. A few had decided to follow Christ and to trust Him for their salvation. I knew my primary roles and responsibility evolved around being wife to my husband and mother to our children. That was true in the States and would be true here.

The team's hard work was seeing some results. Lord, I want to reach out to others and to be able to help them know you in a personal way, too. Show me with whom I can build relationships so that I may be able to share the most beautiful gift that You want to give them—eternal life with You.

Over the next period of months, the Lord began to open opportunities for me to minister to others as I looked. First of all, I approached our landlord's wife to inquire if she would be interested in studying the Bible weekly together. She had already accepted Christ as her Savior, but had had little encounters with other believers regularly nor had she studied the Scriptures on her own. She readily accepted the invitation to paraphrase and discuss the book of John. Naturally, this afforded me regular use of the Italian language conversationally. Developing a strong friendship with an Italian woman gave me further confidence in seeking other friendships.

Directing and accompanying the choir at the Italian Bible Institute was another dramatic challenge. They were kindly patient with my lack of melodic use of their language. However, together we sought to bring praise to the Lord.

The other two staff wives and I began to meet weekly to share in God's Word together and to pray for one another. This type of supportive interaction helped to establish our friendships and to encourage us in our new cultural lifestyle.

November 15, 1981
Dear Mom,

Satan surely desires that we sit in a corner defeated by all the circumstances and lavish pitiful thoughts on ourselves instead of seeing the good in each situation and being able to praise and obey God that day. As soon as a negative thought comes, I try to reject it and replace it with something else. If credence isn't given to negative input into our mental computer, it cannot germinate other devastating thoughts.

Friendships were developing in our apartment complex and in our neighborhood. Our boys were accepted immediately in the play yard and were brought readily into their friends' homes. This created an excellent opportunity to meet many of the families. One friendship was formed by our youngest son, Jon, with Angelo across the hall. As I baked American treats, I would often send some over to Angelo's family, the Berettas. His mom began to send back Italian specialties as well.

I was writing out my testimony in Italian to be presented at a particular meeting and needed it to be corrected for any mistakes. I had helped one of Angelo's sisters regularly with her English, which made me feel comfortable to ask for her help with this. Her mother answered the door telling me that Laura wasn't home, but that she would love to hear it and help me. The Lord provided a special time with Anna to impart some of His work in my life. Salvation through Jesus Christ and His leading us to Italy were included. She listened carefully, showing a great deal of interest, and made me feel at ease with my stumbling Italian.

February 8, 1982

Gleanings from my study in Isaiah have been profitable. I try to study a portion each day, writing the gist of each part and how it applies to me. Then I look at what I have studied and choose what I wish to worship God for that day.

My last study was from Isaiah 28:23-29. God gives knowledge to the farmer to know how to plant and describes the various grains used. The amount of threshing each kernel can take depends on the type of grain. God imparts wisdom to us in plowing, harrowing, leveling, sowing and planting seeds of His truth. He continues with how much crushing of the seed is good and when too much damages.

I thought of Christ, who is the Bread of Life made from the grain of suffering. We are various types of grains that need to be crushed for more useful purpose, but not damaged. I worship you, Father, today for crushing 'grain' for useful purposes (meaning me).

The time before I wrote, *"Today, I worship you, Father, for Jesus, the Stone upon which I build my life. All activity must be*

*in symmetrical design and dependent on Jesus, the Chief Support,
Foundation of all I do, all I am."*   Isaiah 28:14-22.

I will share just one more from Isaiah 28:9-13. *"I worship you, Father, because you choose to utilize stammering lips
of my foreign tongue."* Then, I like to continue to meditate
on these various aspects of God throughout that day.

A new baby was born to the neighbors downstairs. I
decided to bake a cheesecake and deliver it happily to the
family. Thus, a friendship began. The mother desired to
learn how to make the cheesecake, which would strengthen
our friendship and provide times to introduce her to Jesus'
love for her and her family.

As Christmas holidays came, Jesus' birth opened up new
ways to show His love. I regularly shopped at many of the
small family-run shops in our neighborhood. Wrapping
decoratively small gifts of American Christmas cookies
and candies with a thank you note for their services
became another way to show Christ's love. Our Savior's
Gospel message had been enclosed, too. Our Christmas
greetings and brief exchange of holiday cheer added
strength to growing trust and friendships. Conversations
regarding Christ's birth and its impact upon the world were
also ignited. My recipients were the ladies at the clean-
ers, the men at the hardware store, our doorkeepers, and
the family at the corner grocery store. In fact, they sent a
nice gift and note back to our home. We can reach out with
Christ's love to the people we come in contact with everyday.

March 21, 1982
I got home from a team prayer meeting for the tent
campaign we will have in April. Christ is amazing. He suffered so for us. His prayer in John 17 really struck me. He

was praying for me, for all of us, that God would protect us from the evil one and keep us in unity and preserve us in truth.

The very first night of our tent campaign in Nemorense Park, our oldest son desired to be baptized with the new Italian believers.

As the crowd gathered around, he gave testimony in Italian to the fact of having placed his faith in Jesus Christ. He desired to be His disciple. What joy he brought to his parents' hearts!

April 26, 1982

I am sitting in the kitchen with the oven door open trying to keep warm. April has been very cold, especially inside where the walls retain the damp cold. Without heat, it is no fun.

Now the tent campaign is over. Many were talked to and some professions of faith were made. I began praying God would give them ears to hear and eyes to see spiritually.

I talked to one woman who was hurting a great deal— life shattered, husband left ten years ago. She has been living with one man after another, has two children she doesn't want, and whiskey smelled heavily on her breath.

All she desired was another man to live with—and not Jesus. She almost seemed incapable of making any kind of decision, but never would acknowledge any sin in her life. I prayed for her and never saw her again.

Mario, a seventeen-year-old boy began coming every day and every night. In the beginning, he said he belonged to Satan. One night we were talking to him. He was giving his life story and still refusing Christ because he had been left by his parents in the middle of the street in winter as a young child. Someone took him to an orphanage. From six years of age until 15, he prayed to Jesus every night for someone to adopt him. He would stand by the door and watch as others would get to go with a couple—but never him.

Some witness I am. I began to lose control of my motherly emotions and had to quickly get up and go outside for fresh air and a torrent of tears to our Savior. Needless to describe, the churn of emotion welled inside me! I did pray regularly for him, and the last day of the tent, he accepted Christ. He came up and kissed me and called me his sister in Christ. Sandro, our first baptized believer, is going to disciple Mario.

I had asked the Lord to open opportunities for me to be able to share our greatest gift, salvation for an eternity in Jesus Christ. He had provided a variety of occasions to show forth His love. He was faithful to give me creative ideas, and I had to be faithful to follow them.

Spring months took my husband back to the States to emcee the mission conference at our home church. Friends learned of our furniture requirements and gave generously toward our household needs. We shopped a great deal to find the best prices on necessary furniture items. We did buy some second-hand pieces. However, we were able to buy a lovely new divan and chairs. Imagine! Not until we became missionaries were we able to buy and coordinate lovely new household necessities. We can praise our dear Father that we are His children and have brothers and sisters who love and care for us. They are imitating their Father.

Our home was certainly becoming a comfortable "getaway" from the noisy bluster of activity outside. We now had a home to which we could happily invite neighbors and friends. The boys were pleased and didn't hesitate to have in their friends. Our home was shared with many visitors from the States and various Italian friends and team members.

Months were required to put all the finishing touches on our new apartment home. Making curtains, hemming drapes and selecting appropriate light fixtures and lamps completed the necessary homelike atmosphere. A total look was developing. An eye-catching family gallery was added in the hall. The gallery included pictures of grandparents, aunts, uncles and all the various sport teams to which the boys had belonged. They reminded us of the firm stability of the past and promptly stated that we're still firm and stable.

My husband did finally decide that I needed a dishwasher after staying up several evenings until 1 a.m. helping me wash and dry dishes. More frequently, we were serving guests Italian meals, which are composed of several courses.

Our apartment had finally become "home", where we could relax and make ourselves comfortable. We continued to be very involved in reaching out to others, Italian or American, Christian or non-Christian. Housing friends from the States or hosting friends from Italy became regular routine for our family. Our vision was growing as to the extensive spiritual needs of Europe and how He may want us to be involved in further ministry.

REFLECTIONS ON "TRUST AND OBEY"

Doors of ministry opportunities are opened by the Lord Jesus Christ, while the evil one seeks to slam them shut with negative thought patterns.

Why is it important that our focus in life be drawn into oneness with His purpose?

> *"Grace and peace be multiplied to you in the knowledge of God and of Jesus our Lord; seeing that His divine power has granted to us everything pertaining to life and godliness, through the true knowledge of Him who called us by His own glory and excellence."*
>
> II Peter 1:2, 3

Have you been able to share the good news of Jesus with someone today?

Do we need other believers to pray with and to study the Bible? Why?

> *"But encourage one another day after day, as long as it is still called 'Today,' so that none of you will be hardened by the deceitfulness of sin."*   Hebrews 3:13

What does God say about our thought life?

> *"...whatever is true, whatever is honorable, whatever is right, whatever is pure, whatever is lovely, whatever is of good repute, if there is any excellence and if anything worthy of praise, dwell on these things."*
>
> Philippians 4:8

Are there times when life's burdens and stresses seem to be crushing you?

> *"In my distress I called upon the Lord, and cried to my God for help; He heard my voice out of His temple, and my cry for help before Him came into His ears."*
>
> Psalm 18:6

Does it seem that God could bring good out of it?

> *"And we know that God causes all things to work together for good to those who love God, to those who are called according to His purpose."*   Romans 8:28

How is Christ praying for you in John 17?

CHAPTER FOURTEEN

Hospital Hopping
by Dennis

As the firemen stood next to the crushed Honda, they heard a slight cry. Jill was not dead as they supposed. They quickly turned their attention to prying her broken body from the wreckage. She was rushed to a nearby hospital for treatment.

Rome is a city of 4 million people and has a shortage of intensive care beds. One doctor told me that the entire city had only about 40 intensive care beds. Because of the shortage, the beds are very carefully allocated. A patient must not only have a severe injury, but also be judged as within the range of survival. My wife, Jill, fit only the former qualification. Since they did not expect her to survive, they merely stopped the bleeding and put her to the side to die.

Meanwhile, several kilometers away at Villa Clara, our team was having a group Bible study. Our passage for the day was Acts 9:36-43. In this passage, a godly woman named Dorcas falls sick and dies. She was a believer with a great reputation for good deeds and kindness. The apostle Peter was summoned from nearby Joppa to her town of Lydda. Her friends showed Peter the garments she had made for the poor while she lived. Peter, by God's power, turned to the woman's body and said, *"Tabitha, arise...."* Before all, she came back to life. As a result, throughout Joppa, many came to believe.

As we discussed this passage, someone suggested our need for a similar miracle. "If we could show God's power raising someone from the dead, we would find many come to faith in Christ."

At that very moment, God was doing something for Jill. He was sustaining a life the doctors had considered impossible to save. After three hours, she was still breathing and thus, qualified for intensive care. She was transferred, along with our son, Jon, to San Camillo, Europe's largest hospital.

Six-year-old Jon had benefited from the Italian tradition of getting involved. Auto accidents draw a crowd in Italy. The first people on the scene often pull survivors from the wreckage and apply first aid. The response time for ambulance service is notoriously slow. It is not uncommon for the injured to be loaded into cars and taken to the hospital by civilians. Those carrying the injured place a handkerchief in the driver's side window. As it flaps in the breeze, the driver leans on the horn. I have witnessed these "Good Samaritans" swerving through traffic, running red lights and driving on the wrong side of the highway.

Immediately following Jill's accident on the Via Salaria, a woman in a cab approached the scene. She ordered the cab to pull over, and she ran to our mangled orange Honda. Inside she saw two people. One was a woman apparently dead, and the other a young boy conscious in the back seat. Her immediate concern was to remove him from the bloody scene in the front seat. She reached through the shattered back window and carried him to her cab.

Once in the cab, she began to question him in Italian. He responded in fluent Italian with a perfect accent, the envy of our entire family. He, of course, learned to speak by mimicking his friends, while we had learned in language school. One of the woman's questions was this, "Dov'e il Papa?" (Where is your father?). Jon responded, "Non c'e!" "Non c'e!" has two possible interpretations: "He is not here" or "There is no Father." She assumed the second and was deeply saddened. He was a young boy without a father and now his Mother was dead.

She ordered the cab to take them to a place where she could get Jon something to drink. She offered him a Coke, but he wouldn't drink. From the restaurant, she called a friend at the central police dispatch. To her amazement, she found out the woman in the car was still alive. She found out where Jill had been taken and re-entered her cab to take Jon there as well. The first stop for Jill and Jon was Ospedale Policlinico near the University. When it appeared Jill had a chance of survival, she and Jon were transferred to San Camillo, Rome's best trauma care facility.

We thank God for this woman who cared for our son while neither of us could be there with him.

The day after the accident, I returned to San Camillo to see Jill. I was annoyed to discover their visiting hours. Family members were allowed to visit Tuesday, Thursday, Saturday and Sunday for one hour. Only one family member was allowed to go in at a time after donning surgical garb and a mask. While waiting outside of Rianimazione (Intensive Care), I couldn't help but notice the anguish of those around me. Each of us had a loved one behind the door, near death. Some families huddled together, weeping. Others stood with blank stares on their faces. The room did very little to encourage us. There were but a few chairs in the waiting area. We were actually huddled at the end of a first floor lobby. Behind us were the entrance doors and elevators.

As we waited, patients from other buildings were shuttled noisily through the doors. The socialized medical care in Italy did not impress me. Although the doctors were well-trained, the support staff and facilities were lacking. As we watched one patient come through the door on a gurney, I was amazed by the rough handling. One attendant pulled the front and eased <u>it</u> down a ledge. The other end was left free to drop with a thud as the patient nearly bounced off.

The scene at the elevators was also disconcerting. The first-floor call button was out of order. When the attendants had a patient to transfer upstairs, they would bang on the metal door with their fists. The poor patient would almost rise off the pillow, shocked by the sudden noise. As we watched this charade, it would have been humorous had our loved ones not been patients in their care. We looked at each other and shook our heads praying that our loved ones were getting better care.

Another factor contributed to the trauma outside intensive care. The door before us was the only entrance and exit to intensive care. As we waited for our visit, patients would be wheeled past us in various degrees of injury or trauma. Even worse, as we stood waiting, the doors opened to remove those who had died. The covered head struck a core in every heart, because one did not know if the body belonged to them or someone else. To say the least, the waiting area was charged with anxiety.

Finally, the door opened to visitors, one per patient. I entered the drab green outer area and was handed my surgical clothing and mask. I noticed behind a portable partition a body with its head covered. The constant reminder of death was everywhere. On the wall was a hand-written chart with the day's date. Names were listed in two columns, fifteen in each column. Each column represented a row of beds. Jill was in the second bed on the left side. My anxiety level increased as I walked toward the nursing station. The L-shaped room had not permitted me a view of the beds. The nurse approved my entrance, and I turned left for my first glance.

San Camillo's intensive care was not what I expected. As a pastor in the states, I had visited intensive care facilities. None was like this one. The street-level windows were screened and open. The room was extremely hot, obviously not air-conditioned. Passing cars kicked up dust outside the windows. To my amazement, the beds were in a totally open ward. No rooms were designated for individual patients, not even partitions. I found myself viewing 25 to 30 people in various stages of injury and pain. Some were groaning. One let out an occasional scream. Most were on respirators and IVs.

As we stepped into the room, my eyes quickly looked toward the second bed on the left. No, it was the wrong bed. I felt a flash of anger. They couldn't even make the chart right. Maybe bed two was at the other end. I walked the length of the beds quickly. I looked at bed two on my left—it was a man. I looked at bed two on my right—it was an elderly woman. My mind raced back to the body in the entry area. Could she have already died and no one knew I was out in the waiting area?

Somewhat frantic, I went from bed to bed, side to side. Nothing—she wasn't here. I turned to a nurse and said,

"Non c'e!"

"Not here!" She responded, "Who's not here?"

I said, "My wife—she's not here."

"What's her name?" she inquired.

"Jill", I submitted.

"She's here in bed number 2!," the nurse said, pointing to the original bed 2 on the left.

As I walked toward the bed, I was overcome with disbelief. It was Jill, but she bore almost no physical resemblance. Her hair was completely cut off, her face swollen, black and blue. Tubes protruded from her mouth and nose. Her body was covered with numerous cuts and abrasions.

Her right leg was in traction with a metal pin protruding through her knee. Above the knee was a jagged wound that had been sewn together. The bone above the knee had a nauseating sag in it—like a swayback horse. Every part of her body seemed broken or marred in some way. I touched her hand and found no response. I spoke, but received no reaction from my comatose wife. I marveled at her ability to cling to life and then prayed silently to the "Life-giver of all life." I asked for His care—but did not plead for her life. I wanted God's best for her. If life meant pain, suffering and frustration, God's best might include taking her home. I was allowed one hour, but I couldn't take it. After 20 minutes, I left; shaken and amazed by the gravity of Jill's injuries. I returned to find our team in prayer and to news that our pastor and his wife were coming from Dallas to minister to us. My mother and brother were also coming to be with my children. We advised Jill's parents to wait. We reasoned they could be of greater help when Jill came out of the coma. After that first visit, I had to wonder if she ever would come out of the coma.

REFLECTIONS ON HOSPITAL HOPPING

The only time we have to glorify God is right now; we don't know about tomorrow.

When we have no control over circumstances and are bound by our limitations, who is in control?

> *"For who is God, but the Lord? And who is a rock, except our God, the God who girds me with strength and makes my way blameless? He makes my feet like hinds' feet, and sets me upon my high places...You have also given me the shield of your salvation, and Your right hand upholds me and Your gentleness makes me great."*
> Psalm 18:31-33, 35

According to these verses, what does God provide for you?

When something tragic happens to us, does it necessarily mean we have been disobedient to God and He is punishing us?

" As He passed by, He saw a man blind from birth. And His disciples asked Him, 'Rabbi, who sinned, this man or his parents, that he would be born blind?' Jesus answered, 'It was neither that this man sinned, nor his parents; but it was so that the works of God might be displayed in him."   John 9:1-3

CHAPTER FIFTEEN

Squeeze My Hand

by Dennis

My second visit to San Camillo was for information only. On non-visiting days, family members gathered in the lobby just like on visiting days. No information was available by phone. No one had a personal physician. At around noon, a doctor would step outside the door of intensive care. We would form a single-file line and wait for our turn to talk to the doctor. I observed the routine. As each approached the doctor, he would state the patient's name, the doctor would look up, rub his chin and give a response. A follow-up question or two extended the consultation to approximately 45 seconds for each of us. The response was typically, "a little better," "a little worse," or "about the same." When my turn arrived, he said, "She is a little better today." After a one-hour drive across Rome and a 45-minute wait, all I got was a 15-second report. No visit would be allowed until tomorrow.

The next day when I arrived at the hospital, several people were there to meet me. Several missionary friends from Greater European Mission were very encouraging. Our Italian neighbors and friends showed much concern and support. During my visit, I took Jill's hand and spoke to her. I asked her if she could hear me. To my amazement, she squeezed my hand. I repeated my question, and once again, she squeezed my hand.

I motioned for a passing nurse to come to her side. I explained that she was responding to my voice. The nurse took Jill's hand and replied, "Nerves. It's only nerves". I wanted to shout, but for now it was enough that I knew she could hear me. Maybe she would come out of the coma soon, and I could finally see her eyes. As I stood by the bed, several things distressed me. Jill was sweating profusely. The outdoor temperature was in the 90's. She and the other patients were surrounded by a sweat ring on their sheets. Moisture beads ran down her face. I wiped her face dry with a Kleenex tissue. Who wipes her face when I'm not here? I thought. I knew the answer. No one did. While I stood there, Jill turned her head. Immediately, the tube to her respirator fell loose. The respirator alarm started to sound. I quickly reinserted the tube. Who reconnected the tube when I wasn't there? That thought made me break into a cold sweat.

On Saturday, I came for my next visit. As the clock ticked past our visiting time of 12 noon, the group became restless. We only had until 1 p.m. to visit, and our time was slipping away. Finally someone came out to make an announcement: no visitation today. The group was enraged. I pushed to the front and overheard the problem. Not enough nurses had reported for duty. It was a beautiful day and many had gone to the beach. About 15 minutes later, 3 or 4 young volunteers arrived and went into intensive care. Everyone's anxiety level increased a notch. The critical care of our family members was in the hands of teenage volunteers.

A week after the accident, Jill seemed to be stabilizing. Her vital signs were strengthening and she was semi-conscious. Her communication to me was limited to slight pressure on my hand and the blinking of her eyes. She continued on a respirator because of a collapsed lung and broken sternum.

My secretary reminded me that I was being charged for the storage of our wrecked car. I decided to take the time to sign it over because it was a total wreck. As I looked at the little orange Honda Civic, I was once again amazed. The front was crushed almost flat against the firewall. The steering wheel had 2 broken spokes and was 3" from the back of the front seat. The driver's side of the car was folded in like a crushed soft drink can. The front and rear windows were shattered, and the car was littered with glass. A lone sandal lay on the floor amid the dark blood stains. That Jon or Jill survived the impact of the accident was beyond belief.

At 1 p.m., I returned to Via Cimone 100, the location of our team headquarters. I entered the ivy-covered gate and walked up to the three-story Villa. Upon entering the front door, Joanne Eitzen, my secretary, motioned me to one side. "Dennis," she said. "They called after you left San Camillo. Jill has taken a turn for the worse. They said you should come immediately." Joanne said, "Come on. I'll drive." My brother Larry and I rushed out to Joanne's car.

The trip to San Camillo that day seemed like an eternity. The traffic was heavy, and the backups at every intersection were long. We all knew why the hospital had called. It was "the call", the courtesy call made to next of kin. It was made when the doctors believed death was imminent. I wondered if I would see my wife alive again. She had been improving. What had happened? Had someone failed to reconnect her respirator? Had they given her the wrong medication? I was sensing an anger toward this culture — a hatred of the traffic, of socialized medicine, and of the bureaucracy.

As we entered the waiting room, I was greeted by an unexpected sight. Three people were huddled in prayer. They had heard, before me, about Jill's turn for the worse. They had rushed to the hospital to meet me and join me in prayer. They were fellow missionary, Nancy Weynand and Jim and Phyllis Rose. Jim was the pastor of Northwest Bible Church, our home church. We had served on staff at Northwest for almost 10 years. Now we were fully supported missionaries.

When our friends at Northwest heard of Jill's accident, they responded in many ways. This large Dallas church began an emergency medical fund. In two Sundays, they collected over $30,000.00. Many were frustrated by the sketchy information, so they decided to send Jim and Phyllis on the longest hospital call of their lives. The Rose's arrived with a list of prayer supporters that contained over 800 signatures.

Now, at this low moment in my life, I could link arms with my pastor and his wife along with my brother and co-workers. I was indeed privileged to have this support team in Italy and a growing prayer team in the United States. As we joined arms to pray, they gave me the latest news. Jill's blood pressure, which had fallen dangerously low, had once again stabilized. She had survived another day.

REFLECTIONS ON "SQUEEZE MY HAND"

Prayer packs powerful ammunition.

How should one respond in a Christ-like way to injustices?

"...Blessed are you who are poor, for yours is the kingdom of God...But I say to you who hear, love your enemies, do good to those who hate you, bless those who curse you, pray for those who mistreat you."

Luke 6:20, 27, 28

Prayer is a powerful tool of communication. How can we make our praying effective?

"Therefore, confess your sins to one another, and pray for one another so that you may be healed. The effective prayer of a righteous man can accomplish much."

James 5:16

CHAPTER SIXTEEN

Pursuing Another Trip

by Dennis

The sudden turn for the worse changed my opinion about when Jill's parents should come to Rome. I now realized that she could suffer a setback without warning and be gone. I did not want to deprive her parents, Olen and Phyllis Baxter, the privilege of seeing their daughter alive. Two days later, her father, a pastor in Kansas City, and mother arrived. During these days, my mother and brother helped to care for my older sons, Tod and Scot.

Ten days after the accident, my son Jon, 6 years of age at the time, remained in the Pediatric Ward. I was constantly juggling the visitations between Pediatrics and Intensive Care. Sometimes it required hours of sitting outdoors waiting for the next opportunity to see Jill. The 1½ hour round-trip home was impractical. Jon, I was told, was being held for observation. The doctors and nurses in his department were very caring and careful. Jon, of course, pleaded to go home. He felt fine and wanted out. After each visit, I had to turn my back on a tearful child holding outstretched arms toward me. Finally, after several more X-rays, the doctors were satisfied. No head injury and no internal bleeding could be detected. Upon arriving home, he was surprised that Mom was not there. I cautiously explained that Mom's injuries were more serious than his. "She will need to stay in the hospital longer." The possibility of her death didn't seem a wise subject for a young child who had already endured so much trauma.

Jill's parents' first visit to San Camillo was a shock. Jill's physical appearance was brutal—compared to her normal beauty and cheerful countenance. They were sustained by God's grace and were a real source of encouragement to us. One day, Jill's father had an idea. He laid a pad of paper on Jill's chest and placed a pen in her only working hand. By now, two weeks after the accident, she was becoming increasingly alert. She responded slowly, writing the words, I love you, Dad. The letters were far from perfect, but they were legible. We were all encouraged by this appropriate and endearing response. Perhaps the head injury that had left her paralyzed on the left side had not destroyed her ability to think.

From the outset, our Italian doctor, Dr. Stopanni, advised us to take Jill back to the United States. The Italian health care system has fine doctors, but poor support. The intensive care wing in Italy's largest hospital was without needed air-conditioning and lacked modern equipment. The Socialized System was very unresponsive to communicating with the patient's family. Jill had no assigned physician and, thus, we had no point of contact. It was impossible to get information by phone, and no one ever called back.

Jill's father, Olen, and I busied ourselves trying to get Jill back to the States. We are both aggressive and determined by nature.

Day after day we hit brick walls. The hospital would not assist us. They said a move was too dangerous and would risk her life. Yet, we knew that we wanted her leg surgery and therapy completed in the States.

One day we visited the American Embassy to see if they would help. The Ambassador's assistant was very sensitive and sympathetic. He pledged to help in any way possible. He then sent me to the administrator, a Mr. Montenegro. Mr. Montenegro had served with the American Embassy for over 15 years. His first statement was to the effect, "Now let us talk about reality." He handed us a sheet of paper. The sheet listed the criteria necessary for Embassy assistance to American civilians. We didn't qualify for a military airlift and so that was that. We left the embassy totally frustrated. We had exhausted every possibility. The commercial airlines would transport her, but only with a release from the hospital. Midway through week three after the accident, we were at a dead-end.

Five days later, the phone rang. "Dr. Eenigenburg," Mr. Montenegro from the Embassy began. "I want to give you an update on your wife's condition." I was shocked. He continued, "I will speak to the Primario at San Camillo daily and then give you an update." What a change! Why was he involved after brushing us off a few days earlier? The next day he said the Primario at the hospital would like to see me tomorrow. The Primario was the head of Intensive Care. He was an important person at the hospital. His position was one of status and power. He called the shots and made decisions. If we could get his cooperation, we could fly Jill to the States. But we didn't even know why we had been granted an audience with him, let alone his attitude toward our request.

The next day, my father-in-law and I and the director of our mission, Royal Peck, sat outside the Primario's office at San Camillo. Each of us had our questions ready.

Finally, we were invited into a large office with traditional high ceilings. The room was somewhat stark. The marble floors always caused a resonance to footsteps and conversations. My father-in-law began questioning as Royal interpreted. "Why are we restricted to four visits per week? She is aware now. She needs to know we are here for her." The Primario leaned back in his chair with a knowing smile on his face.

"I'm sorry, sir, but it's too much work for her to have visitors." He called me forward, "Dammi tuo mano," (Give me your hand). With a ball-point pen he drew a line across the knuckle of my index finger. "Pretend," he said, "this were a cut on your finger. Now bend your finger. Would the cut finger feel better still, or bending?"

"Still," I replied.

"Exactly!" he bellowed triumphantly. "That is what feels best for your wife's brain, to be still, to rest. That's why we only allow four visits per week." We tried to counter with arguments about exercising her brain, but to no avail.

We changed topics to one we were most concerned about. When can we take her back to the United States? A friend, Dr. Phil Williams in Dallas, was prepared to travel with her if necessary. "It's out of the question," he said. "She is much too weak." Leaving the office, we all felt disappointed. We had made no progress toward getting her released.

The bright spot of that week was Jon's release from the hospital. He was delighted to see his brothers and sleep in his own bed. One afternoon, he accompanied his two grandmothers to a small grocery store. The store was across from our apartment and operated by a very friendly family. Jon translated the names on the packages as they shopped. During the shopping, a young man approached them and greeted them in English.

The young man had heard them speaking and inquired, "I assume you are Americans? This is not a tourist area, why are you here?" They explained briefly the details of Jill's accident. They pointed out our apartment across the street.

"Oh," he responded, "It's nice to meet you. My name is Jamie. I'm from Boston. I'm sorry that you are here under such difficult circumstances. I've noticed the three blonde-headed boys when I walk home from school. I live a short distance up the street." "By the way," he added, "I'm a fourth-year medical student here in Rome. If I can ever help you in any way, please call me. Here is my phone number." They thanked him for his concern and finished their shopping. This encounter proved to be more significant than any of us would have imagined.

Two days later, the phone rang. It was the American Embassy.

"Mr. Eenigenburg, San Camillo called me this morning. Your wife needs surgery on her leg. They believe she is stable enough to endure surgery. If you want it done here, they will do it. But she should also remain here for after-care. If you want her surgery done in the United States, they suggest you move her in the next day or two. One more thing, Mr. Eenigenburg, if you check her out, you must sign a document. The document will say they did not recommend her traveling to the United States. If she doesn't make it, you will be solely responsible. They think she will make it, but do not want the responsibility."

After I hung up, I let out a shout, "Finally!" The family gathered quickly. "We can fly her home. San Camillo will release her." During the next eight hours, my father-in-law and I were all over Rome making preparations and placing calls across the Atlantic.

TWA had a non-stop flight from Rome to New York. We hated the idea of going through JFK, but it could not be helped. We contacted TWA in Rome, and they called their headquarters in Kansas City. Yes, flight 841 could be rigged for a stretcher. There were guidelines, however. A six-page medical report had to be filled out in English by her attending physicians in Rome. Secondly, she had to be accompanied by a doctor who would take full responsibility for her care. Thirdly, the stretcher, the doctor and the equipment would require four first-class seats one way to Dallas. The tickets would cost about $6,000.00.

As we sought to meet these requirements, the pieces fell into place. Our home church had escrowed over $30,000.00 for Jill's care. They were more than willing to pay for our flight back to Dallas. A close friend in Dallas, Bob Evans, was a travel agent. He agreed to wire the money to TWA.

There were several doctors in Dallas who offered to fly to Rome to accompany us. Unfortunately, most American doctors do not specialize in trauma care. After residency, they specialize in other types of treatment. The doctor we needed came from an unsuspecting place—San Camillo. The doctor who treated Jill three weeks earlier was a young doctor name Paulo Consoli. He was an anesthesiologist and specialized in trauma care. Unlike the US, Italian doctors specialize in Intensive Care.

Paulo had been planning to go to San Francisco in two weeks. He was taking a one-month study leave. When the Primario found out we wanted to take Jill to Dallas, he suggested Paulo. "I'll let him leave a week early," he told us. "Paulo has flown eight or ten people across the Atlantic for medical treatment." We talked to Paulo, and he agreed to help us. We found Paulo to be a very kind and competent physician. He spoke of Jill as a real person—a person he had grown to care about over the last three weeks. My father-in-law enjoyed the fact that Paulo spoke English quite well.

With two pieces in place, we were left with six pages of medical forms. These forms were facing us with a real dilemma. My 2-1/2 years in Italy had enabled me to learn the language and vocabulary related to everyday life. I had no idea how to translate the information from Italian medical reports to English for TWA. I found that missionaries of twenty years couldn't do it either. We approached Paulo with our problem. He said, "I'm sorry, but I don't know the English words for these Italian terms."

TWA wouldn't budge. No papers, no approval to fly. Then it dawned on me. "What about Jamie, the medical student?" I rushed home, hoping we hadn't thrown his phone number away.

Feverishly, I rustled through the papers on my desk. I found his number and dialed. "We've never met," I started, "but you have met my son, mother and mother-in-law."

He immediately responded in a positive way. "How's your wife?" he asked. I explained our problem. We need someone with an Italian and English medical vocabulary.

"You've found the right man," he replied, "How can I help?"

During the next two days, Jamie made three trips to San Camillo and three trips to TWA. TWA officials in Kansas City reviewed Jill's status and approved her travel. We have marveled at God's timing. Jamie had lived across from us for two years. We never met him until we couldn't have done without him.

REFLECTIONS ON PURSUING ANOTHER TRIP

God can articulate and produce what is needed in the harmful stretches of life when man has no knowledge or authority.

Waiting for God's timing in disastrous situations is difficult. What should our resolve be?

"I would have despaired unless I had believed that I would see the goodness of the Lord in the land of the living. Wait for the Lord; be strong and let your heart take courage; yes, wait for the Lord." Psalm 27:13, 14

God is omniscient where our range of vision is so limited. Must we be trapped by our lack of foresight?

" Trust in the Lord with all your heart and do not lean on your own understanding. In all your ways acknowledge Him, and He will make your paths straight."
Proverbs 3:5, 6

CHAPTER SEVENTEEN

Miles of Miracles

by Dennis

Flight preparations were quite complicated. I had become accustomed to snags in the Italian bureaucracy. I told my father-in-law, "I'll not relax until that 747 lifts off from the tarmac at Leonardo Da Vinci."

Paulo requested a large suitcase the night before we were to leave. In it, he would carry all of the supplies and medications needed. He also packed a respirator. Jill was still unable to breathe on her own. TWA assured us that it would have an ample supply of oxygen for the ten-hour flight to New York.

Bob Evans in Dallas wired the money to TWA in Rome so our tickets could be written. Because of the 7-hour time change, we only had one hour to do our transfer. The telex was delayed, and the ticket office in Rome closed as we waited.

The agent suggested we come back in the morning— the morning of the flight. "No!" I insisted, "We want the tickets in hand tonight."

They said, "Fine, but we leave in thirty minutes. If the approval does not come, we can't write the tickets." We paced and prayed.

Ten minutes passed, then twenty. I heard the telex machine begin. Tickets approved. The two agents looked disappointed—they were going to have to work late. Over 15 individual tickets had to be handwritten. An hour later, with tickets in hand, we headed for my apartment. All of us were ready early the next morning. My mother was taking our three sons with her to Chicago. They were going directly to Leonard Da Vinci, the Rome airport. Jill's appearance was still very bad. She had lost weight and could not talk. The boys had not seen Jill, and we wanted to protect them from the emotional strain. They would travel on Alitalia. We would be on TWA #841.

Russ Rosser, president of Christ's Mission, had come to Rome because of Jill's accident. He and Royal Peck had assigned my responsibility as team director to my assistant director, Bo Wilks. Since the transition of leadership had been worked out, he was returning with us to New York. He and my mother-in-law went directly to the airport with our luggage. My father-in-law and I went to the hospital to accompany Jill to the plane.

When we arrived at the intensive care wing, tensions were high. We could hear the Primario yelling at someone. That someone turned out to be Paulo. He had worked all night and was now in trouble with his Chief of Staff. We found out later what he had done to offend his boss. He had been sent to the Primario's residence to pick up a respirator in a case.

Actually, he found two respirators and took one of them. His chief was upset because he'd taken the wrong one. He was to take the one with the Primario's name on the side. The Primario wanted the doctors in the United States to see his name. I recognized the importance of "bella figura" in Italy, but this was too much. We were concerned about Jill's life and he about his reputation. In retrospect, we are very thankful that the Italians kept Jill alive. We have never doubted their genuine skillful effort on her behalf.

As Jill was transmitted to the ambulance, an attendant kept her breathing with an Ambue bag. The ambulance had one of the sophisticated life-support equipment found in the States. As we sped toward the airport on the Raccordo Anulare, something puzzled me. Why had the American Embassy become interested in Jill? What influenced the Primario to change his mind about moving Jill? I only knew at the time that many hundreds of people were praying for Jill and her well-being.

Two months later, I discovered the mechanism that God had triggered in response to prayer.

Bob Hyde was a friend of ours from Northwest Bible Church who worked for a major electronics firm in Dallas. When Bob heard of Jill's accident, he sought more information. Gradually, our struggles with the bureaucracy filtered back to Dallas. He heard the Embassy was unresponsive, and that we couldn't get Jill released to come to the States. Bob decided to call a friend from the Pentagon, General Click Smith. This General was a committed Christian and very sympathetic to Jill's situation. He told Bob that, officially, there was little he could do, but that he and others would join in prayer for Jill.

General Smith's concern led him to contact the Embassy in Rome. He informed the Embassy of his interest in Jill and requested a daily update of her condition. When the Pentagon became interested in Jill, the American Embassy became interested. And when the Pentagon was concerned for Jill's well-being, the Italian government-run hospital became much more concerned. The last thing they wanted was someone important to the US government dying while in their care. What they wanted was good public relations and, thus, the wheels began to move.

The Embassy called the hospital daily and reported Jill's condition to me and to the Pentagon. The hospital contacted me and began to work with us to return her to the United States and out of their liability.

Later, we found another reason the Embassy was so responsive to the General. This General had a special task. He was in charge of the safety of all American Embassy personnel worldwide. If a threat to the safety of the Rome Embassy Personnel erupted, this General would coordinate their evacuation or rescue. If there was one General they wanted to keep happy, it was Bob Hyde's General friend at the Pentagon.

When the ambulance arrived at the Leonardo Da Vinci airport, we hit another snag. The security officials would not allow the ambulance to enter the tarmac. Several years earlier, terrorists had used an ambulance as a disguise and had killed several people. We had to wait for a Red Cross ambulance and transfer her to that vehicle. Then, accompanied by Security Police, we approached the TWA 747 sitting outside the terminal.

Jill's stretcher was loaded into the food service truck next to the plane. The doctor and two attendants joined her as the bed was raised to the service door. Throughout the trip from the hospital, Dr. Consoli continued to respirate Jill with an Ambue bag. Once aboard the plane, he would reattach a respirator for our long trip across the Atlantic. I climbed the passenger stairs and found Jill's parents already on board. On the right side of the first class section, two seat-beds had been collapsed forward. Over these seats, next to the wall, a cot-like bed had been hung.

The ambulance attendants laid her on the cot and returned to their ambulance. Dr. Consoli, still working the Ambue bag, asked a hostess for the oxygen the airline promised to provide.

I had told my father-in-law that when we lifted off for the US, I would be able to relax. We had all been driven by adrenalin for weeks. Unfortunately, the tension was not over. The hostess returned with a long thin oxygen bottle, the kind used for assisting individuals with emphysema or other breathing disorders. It was totally inadequate to run our respirator. The airline had misunderstood the kind of oxygen tanks we needed. Now we were faced with a dilemma. We would have to respirate Jill by hand for the next 12-15 hours. It was either that or get off the plane, and that we were not about to do.

As we lifted off, Dr. Consoli motioned to me. "She's breathing on her own!"

"Thank God," we replied. For the first time in almost four weeks, she was breathing unaided.

As we traveled toward our first stop, New York, Dr. Consoli continued to monitor Jill's vital signs. Periodically, he would give her water through a nose tube that went into her stomach. She seemed to be taking the trip very well.

Four hours out over the Atlantic, a normally calm doctor beckoned me to his side. "Hold this up," he said with urgency in his voice. It was a cardiac catheter still imbedded in her chest. Paulo quickly opened a suitcase full of pharmaceuticals and syringes and inserted a needle into the rubber top of a bottle full of clear fluid. He carefully drew out a measured amount. Turning toward Jill, he inserted the needle into the tube I was holding. I knew something was wrong, but I also knew it was not the time to ask. Paulo quickly placed his stethoscope on her arm and began monitoring her heart.

Later, in Dallas, Paulo related the gravity of those minutes. Jill had quickly lost blood pressure. He had to give her a cardiac stimulant to keep her heart beating. I was glad he hadn't told me earlier.

Our six-hour layover in New York was like a lifetime. We were met by the wrong kind of ambulance and attendants that wandered off when we needed their help to reboard the plane. Airline workers, who argued about who was to set up the stretcher, delayed us unnecessarily for an extra hour.

Twenty hours after leaving Rome, we arrived in Dallas. When the commissary door opened, I was never so relieved in my life. There was our personal friend and skilled neurosurgeon, Phil Williams. Dr. Williams was accompanied by his nurse, Barbara, and an associate, Dr. Nardizzi. It was 11 p.m. Dallas time, and Phil was ready and waiting. When we arrived at Presbyterian Hospital, five more doctors were waiting in the Emergency Room.

I'd waited for doctors my entire life, but had never had them wait for me. They were there as a favor to Dr. Williams, and we deeply appreciated their care in the following months. We were to benefit greatly from several in particular: Dr. Roby Mize, a brilliant orthopedic surgeon, and Dr. Russ Sparenberg who treated some deep bed sores.

Two and one-half years after leaving for our mission to Italy, we were back in Dallas. It was good to be home again, but it was also somewhat confusing. Why send us and then bring us back? God has yet to answer that question. But then, He is God and isn't obligated to answer all my questions. What is clear to me is that when we go for Him, He goes with us—even to the end of this life. When death becomes the next event, it will be a doorway to eternal life.

If God had taken Jill to be with Him through death, He would not have been less faithful. He would have just expressed His love in another way. God is trustworthy, and the gift of salvation in Jesus Christ proves His love for all. Adversity is not what we ask for, but when it comes, God will either give us the grace to endure, or will, in His mercy, relieve the pain. I thank God for giving me back my wife from the edge of death. It has helped me not to take life for granted and to focus on the things that are important.

About a month before the accident, Jill and I bought two rose bushes. I bought one that was about 10" high. She bought one about 2" high. I asked her, "Why did you pick that one? It will never bloom this year."

She said, "Because I liked the color on the tag."

I planted them both on our balcony. One day, while Jill was in the hospital in Rome, I walked out on the patio to think. Those days were really tough. I glanced down, and to my amazement, Jill's little bush had its first flower—a beautiful crimson blossom. As I looked at that plant, I remembered my statement, "That rose won't bloom this year!" But there it was, beautifully alive. Then I remembered what the doctors said about Jill. She is not expected to make it through the night. But she was alive. As I looked at the rose, I knew why she had survived. She was in the hands of the same God that made the rose bush bloom.

She was in the care of the God of the Rose.

REFLECTIONS ON MIRACLES

Man's attempts to sustain life are superceded by the One who gives the breath of life.

Dealing with life's problems, we usually rely on self to solve the hurricanes of horror that hover over us. What is Christ's invitation?

> *"Come to Me, all who are weary and heavy-laden, and I will give you rest. Take My yoke upon you and learn from Me, for I am gentle and humble in heart, and you will find rest for yours souls. For My yoke is easy and My burden is light."*   Matthew 11:28-30

Describe God's character from Psalm 36:5, 6.

> *"Your lovingkindness, O Lord, extends to the heavens, Your faithfulness reaches to the skies. Your righteousness is like the mountains of God; Your judgments are like a great deep. O Lord, You preserve man and beast."*

These qualities also should be reflected in us if we are God's child. How are they being developed in your life?

> *"He will bring forth your righteousness as the light and your judgment as the noonday."*   Psalm 37:6

Jesus performed many miracles in the Gospels. The greatest miracle He has performed for each of us is stated in Luke 5:23, 24.

> *"Which is easier, to say, 'Your sins have been forgiven you,' or to say, 'Get up and walk'? But, so that you may know that the Son of Man has authority on earth to forgive sins,"—He said to the paralytic—"I say to you, get up, and pick up your stretcher and go home."*

Jesus is responding to the scribes and Pharisees doubting His authority as God. What is the miracle He has already accomplished for you?

CHAPTER EIGHTEEN

Where Am I?

by Jill

The 7th of August I remember well. Lying in my hospital room, looking around and seeing the traffic of white uniforms in the halls, I was frustrated that I was speaking in English to the nurses. Of course, they could only understand Italian. Next time, to be sure, I would respond in Italian if they spoke to me in Italian. No one did. I kept waiting. Questions were arising in my mind. Those were doctors and nurses. This is a hospital room, and those are hospital corridors outside my door.

"Honey," I whispered intently to my husband, peering into his eyes. "What am I doing in a hospital? Why am I here?"

Dennis simply stated the basic facts, expanding on them more carefully in the days that followed, as I probed. I appreciated his wisdom in slowly unfolding the story according to what I could digest.

From the time of the accident, I had not been aware of what was happening. On this very day, my awareness was opening up, and a new picture was unfolding before me. My husband related that I had been flown out of Italy to Dallas, Texas, and was in the Presbyterian Hospital where I had given birth to our sons. I did not need to speak Italian to the doctors and nurses. They would not be able to understand. "Oh! That is why they mostly speak English!" I thought.

Thankfully, the Lord God did not let me be aware of all the ugly, difficult things that had happened. I am glad that has not been a noose hanging around my neck. Our Father is gracious.

A special bed had been given me to use. It was high, and the mattress full of air-blown sand created especially to decrease bed sores and to aid in the healing of the operation I had already had on my lower back to remove an enormous bed sore. To my surprise, I learned that I could not climb out of bed. I could not walk. No weight was to be put on my legs. Such a helpless feeling comes to not be able to use the bathroom or to look through your drawers or go to the closet. I had no idea what I would even find. Already gowns and other items were surrounding me that I had never seen before or chosen.

Where did these items come from? I learned then that many friends and family members had given me lovely gowns, bed jackets, slippers, panties and books. A multitude of floral arrangements crowned the room, bringing fresh aromas of God's lovely creation. To be loved and cared for helps one recover, even though I did feel a bit out of control of my life.

The main character of this particular drama was ME. Yet, I knew none of the scenes in which I had been a participant. Everyone else seemed to know more about my life than I did! Frustrations clamored within me. I also had to accept many new physical limitations and work to continue to better myself through physical therapy. It was comforting to be handed an occasional item that had been originally mine. It was mine—before all of this happened. And I was still me.

One day a friend brought me the most beautiful, feminine eyelet gown and jacket I believe I have ever seen; so delicate, wistful, yet sweet, in its cotton white. Another friend made a lovely soft blue spaghetti-strapped nightgown. Several sent a special Neiman-Marcus tray of delicious luncheon foods for us to enjoy. A friend who had been a teacher at my son's school surprised me with a petite cross-stitched plaque saying, "With God, all things are possible." Lovely memories.

Several friends took turns coming to spend the nights with me. I did not care to be left on my own in this whole new situation without some "protection." Because I could hardly do anything for myself, I felt a need for someone to personally oversee my needs. Their faithfulness afforded me peace and good nights' rest. My back and feet would be rubbed, my fingernails painted, my eyebrows plucked, my legs shaved. These female activities helped me to feel more like my old self and more acceptable to be with. One special elderly couple lovingly desired to take on the project of mounting my hundreds of cards and letters in a scrapbook.

I was the fortunate recipient of school children's letters of concern and gifts from friends in other countries, making it clear to me that my Father had honored their prayers and was taking care of me. My Lord Jesus loves me. He loves you.

I continued taking physical therapy for the strengthening and future use of my legs as well as occupational therapy for my left arm to increase its mobility and use. My husband sketched the doctor's plan for my recovery. I would pray and do all I could to accomplish those goals.

My husband was by my side at the hospital every day, ready to help in any way needed. He would encourage me, giving all the support one could ask for from one's life partner. Willingly, he performed many tasks that I would never have wanted him to have to do for me in my lifetime.

I was getting better as I went to therapy. My limbs worked toward their maximum ability, always striving to increase mobility. Improvement was coming.

REFLECTIONS ON DISPLACEMENT

Contemplating God's ordained change of plans points to His sovereignty.

I Corinthians 13 describes God's love. Write out the attributes of His love. How are you displaying these qualities in your life?

Can you expect to do it by yourself?

> *"For to me, to live is Christ and to die is gain."*
> Philippians 1:21

Thankfully, His Spirit indwells us when we accept Him as Savior.

"But if the Spirit of Him who raised Jesus from the dead dwells in you, He who raised Christ Jesus from the dead will also give life to your mortal bodies through His Spirit who dwells in you."   Romans 8:11

What is a recent example of someone loving you in a Christ-like manner?

Give an example of your loving care for someone when it was undeserved.

Why was Christ essential in my recovery?

"I can do all things through Him who strengthens me."
Philippians 4:13

CHAPTER NINETEEN

Happy Anniversary

by Jill

Four days after I'd become cognizant of what had happened, my husband arranged to celebrate our 15th wedding anniversary on the top floor of the hospital. It was fairly bare of decor and encased by windows. A young man, who had come to trust the Lord as his Savior some years earlier during Dennis' youth ministry, provided all of the lovely accessories and food for a romantic candle-light dinner. However, I was not feeling very romantic as I was doing well to sit up and eat. I felt weak, but grateful that I was here to enjoy my husband. I loved him and was very thankful for his devoted care of me.

He came regularly to the hospital each morning and stayed with me throughout each day, wheeling me to therapy and caring for my needs. The weekend after I had become aware of my new circumstances, the doctors gave permission for an excursion. My husband carefully transported me and my new companion-chair down the many halls and elevators out to the enormous covered parking lot. Carefully, he lifted me into the front seat, buckling the belt, and then pushed the chair to the trunk for storage; this was to become the regular pattern for months to come. Nearby, we approached a lovely restaurant, which provided an excellent palatable change from hospital foods. The Mexican dish of nachos proved to be an outstanding appetizer. Being wheeled, however, out in public was a new experience. One senses that you are a spectacle—certainly to be observed. People were very helpful and kind, but you know that you are different. However, going out for dinner became a regular treat in the following weeks.

During this time of learning the events in my life that had taken place, I asked, "But what about Mike and Kathy?"

"They are in Italy right now speaking to the team for conference," my husband informed me.

"No, that couldn't be! That couldn't be! Right now? We were supposed to be there hosting them and showing them all of Rome. I had my whole menu planned. They couldn't be in Rome without us."

Oh, how I had looked forward to having them in our home. The previous year, Dennis had invited them to speak at our annual conference. We'd double-dated in college and were in seminary together. We had long looked forward to having them as our guests.

The following weekend, I again had permission to spend time away from the hospital. I was going to see our three sons at a very dear friend's home. They served us a lovely dinner. I was glad to be there—to be alive—even if it meant observing the boys swimming from my wheelchair inside the house. I did not wheel myself where I wanted, as my left arm and hand were very weak. Getting to be with the boys again, though, was excellent! I could hug and kiss them and send them off to Mother's to begin school. That was good—and difficult They will be starting in a new school and city without me. Ugh! "Lord, help them be strong—and me, too, Father."

I looked forward to going to the home of a special elderly couple the next weekend. The gentleman led singing at church with a great deal of zest and gusto in God's honor. His wife would accompany beautifully, too; they were a team. I desired to be rolled up to their big black grand piano and play, expressing myself fully on the keyboard. With hands in position, I pressed the keys, waiting for a sound. Again I pressed...I tried again...and again to offer some melodious sonnet. Nothing came. Darkness crept over me. I was stunned. I had played the piano all my life and had taught a number of students. Not even a sound would come! I know that everyone felt the anguish for me; they were wanting me to play as badly as I wanted to. Was this the end of my life? Was I defeated? I knew I needed to wait—and not jump to any rash conclusions. There were many other mountains to climb and capture first. I must save my energy for them. If it's your will, Lord, let me play again.

The doctors had decided that I could begin to walk in therapy if I had a cast put on my entire leg. I had always hated the idea of casts and certainly had not changed that opinion at this point. A big heavy piece of plaster to lug around was not appealing; the wheelchair seemed better.

A cast was formed around my leg, intending to give me the support I would need to walk. My leg could not have weight put upon it yet. There were ten screws in a metal plate inside my leg to reconstruct the femur area. The bone transplant needed to heal completely. The cast was dreadful and caused great discomfort.

Due to the constant pain when walking, the doctor decided to have it removed and replaced with another. The second cast did not prove to be much better. After a couple of days, it was also removed. Relief and joy returned. I would wait until my leg healed.

REFLECTIONS ON CELEBRATIONS

God allows limitations to launch us into new arenas of dependence on Him.

One faces many events in life. Philippians 4:4 tells us, *"Rejoice in the Lord always...again, I will say, rejoice!"* Why is this practical when things aren't going as you planned?

Who is our joy directed to?

Roadblocks in life challenge us. Who tears them down?

> *"...For by You I can run upon a troop; and by my God I can leap over a wall."*   Psalm 18:29

CHAPTER TWENTY

Going Home!
by Jill

Early September, 1982, brought my release from the hospital. Our flight to Kansas City, Missouri was scheduled. For the school year, we would live with my parents and eighteen-year-old brother. They graciously had taken in our sons, and now were gladly receiving my husband and me. School had already started. The boys had made the adjustment. Finally, I was home! We could be a family again!

Dennis helped me get ready and pack for our trip. Being wheeled into the airport seemed strange as was being wheeled around the metal detector and frisked. We did get to board the plane early, which helped. My stomach was tied in a dozen knots.

How would things be at Mom's? What would people think of me? Those thoughts were coupled with joyful excitement—to be home with the ones I loved. That's where I had always been, and that is where I belonged. No sooner had we boarded the plane when I asked my husband to wheel me to the bathroom. Hopefully, this would give me the relief I was needing. Thankfully, few were on the plane. He graciously served in this way, carrying me back to my seat. Not long after the plane had been filled with travelers and had ascended into the skies, I needed to visit the restroom again. Poor husband. In front of everyone, he had to carry me inconspicuously to the restroom, wait for my call and carry me back to my seat. I decided that regardless of my inclinations and churning stomach, I would wait until we arrived home.

Arrival at the airport was exhilarating. Gratefully, I was wheeled off to see the familiar faces of those I loved. Anticipation had been running high, and hugs and kisses flowed.

Soon we arrived at Mom and Dad's. What was going to be the best route to get Jill safely carted inside? Dad told Dennis to wheel me around the house. We arrived at the backside of the home to see the family standing there with smiling faces, proudly displaying the excellent gray ramp they had built up to the porch for their mother's triumphal entry. A perfect act of love that proved to be a big help.

Mom and Dad's home was the very best place for me to recuperate. They had cared for me for years and certainly were not about to stop now. Our room was ready for us and a lovely meal prepared to say, "Welcome Home." My baby grand had been stored at Mother's while I was in Italy. I was wheeled up to the piano and with not much difficulty, began playing. Delight filled my heart. With therapy, my arms and hands had gained the needed strength to be able to play again. Thank you, Lord!

I had to begin to function as I could in my new surroundings and accept my limitations. So badly I longed to walk in the kitchen and help Mother fix our meals or launder our clothes. The confinement to my "chair" grieved me when I could not even help clear the table after a meal or help with the dishes. Everyone had to wait on me, serve me and pamper me. They did so willingly, and I had no choice.

My life had been centered around making meals for others and serving their needs. This was a new me. A different me. Who was I?

I had seen progress coming slowly through the past weeks. At least I was here, and I could kiss each of my sons good-bye as they went off to school. Thank you, Father. I had to begin to accept my limitations, which certainly motivated me to want to get started in therapy so that one day I could walk again.

My husband took me to the rehabilitation center. I would meet my new therapists, an activity I did not look forward to. What if our personalities did not mesh? They may not be nearly as nice or as understanding as the ones in Dallas. Frightened and feeling awkward, I was wheeled into these new surroundings with new faces and new smells. We waited patiently for my first session to begin.

Meeting my therapists that week and beginning our sessions together was uplifting. They seemed to know what they were doing and were sensitive to who I was as a person. Being a therapist requires a special ability to be patient and caring for their clients. The sessions seemed practical and productive. I was glad to be under their care.

Before the accident had taken place, I had been studying the book of Isaiah in the Old Testament. I certainly had time now each day to revel in its pages which continuously show the fullness of God the Father, His wisdom and power. I needed His words daily to heal me inwardly and to keep me strong and growing.

Do you not know? Have you not heard? The everlasting God, the Lord, the creator of the ends of the earth does not become weary or tired. His understanding is inscru-

table. He gives strength to the weary. And to him who lacks might He increases power. And vigorous young men stumble badly yet those who wait for the Lord will gain new strength; They will mount up with wings like eagles they will run and not get tired. They will walk and not become weary. Isaiah 40:28-31

Poignant promises of our Father's power and care for those who wait for Him are revealed in Isaiah. I needed His healing words.

After our Christmas celebration that year, my husband and I flew to Dallas to have day surgery on my leg. My leg had healed, allowing the screws and metal strips to be removed. Another step towards victory. Waiting at least six more weeks for proper bone enclosures where the metal had been was necessary before beginning to put weight on my leg.

Yes, it did heal. Yes, I could begin to put weight on my leg fully. I had started using a walker, but now I could begin to walk using a cane for a bit of added support. With the therapist's help, I soon was able to begin walking alone.

It was not a beautifully conducted walk with perfect agility, but it was a beginning towards more independence. Clearing the table, washing dishes and doing laundry were now a part of my schedule again. What a privilege to be able to work—to be able to care for my family again.

REFLECTIONS ON GOING HOME

The joy of being a family is modeled to us by the Father, the Son, the Holy Spirit, and God's children— the church.

Where is your home?

> *"Therefore, being always of good courage, and knowing that while we are at home in the body we are absent from the Lord..."*   II Corinthians 5:6

> *"The earth is the Lord's, and all it contains, the world, and those who dwell in it."*   Psalm 24:1

Is your present home capable of maintaining its functions for eternity?

> *"The earth mourns and withers, the world fades and withers, the exalted of the people of the earth fade away."*   Isaiah 24:4

Do you have a new home already paid in full and designed for eternity?

> *"In My Father's house are many dwelling places; if it were not so, I would have told you; for I go to prepare a place for you. If I go and prepare a place for you, I will come again and receive you to Myself, that where I am, there you may be also. And you know the way where I am going."*   John 14:2-4

Do you know the way to your new home?

> *"Jesus said to him, 'I am the way, and the truth, and the life; no one comes to the Father by through Me."*
>
> John 14:6

CHAPTER TWENTY-ONE

Victory in Repercussions

by Jill

In spring of 1983, our home church, Northwest Bible Church in Dallas, Texas, asked my husband to come back as associate pastor. For us, this would be going home. We were thrilled to be invited and pleased to accept. At this time, we had a perfect peace that this was our Father's will for us. We would be just as much in the center of God's will in Dallas, Texas, as we had been in Rome, Italy.

The boys were delighted to get to move back home again. When the school year ended, we moved to Dallas. Dennis had gone back to Rome earlier to have our furniture and household items shipped back to the States. We were truly going home!

> *When you pass through the waters I will be with you; and though the rivers, they will not overflow you. When you walk through the fire, you will not be scorched. Nor will the flame burn you. For I am the Lord your God The Holy One of Israel, your Savior;*
>
> Isaiah 43:2,3

The Lord had taken care of us and had provided abundantly beyond all we could imagine or dream. He had restored my health. I could walk now. I could play the piano again. And I could care for our family and myself again.

He had brought us back to our home in Dallas with our church family, as well. Thankfulness became a constant commodity.

Some repercussions, however, still demand reckoning with. My voice is no longer as clear and strong. Permanent damage was done to the vocal chords.

People always ask if I'm suffering from a cold or have laryngitis. No longer can I sing as well as I once did, nor can I always be heard when I desire to be. Frustration sets in and seeks to strangle the thankfulness that must continue to praise my Lord God that I can even talk.

The left side of my body has spasticity, which is the result of having been paralyzed. My left hand will not respond as quickly at the keyboard as it once did. A few exercises help decrease the spasticity, its tightness and rigidity.

I have been learning to appreciate and facilitate my good right hand with its capabilities. The left hand may come along and assist as it will.

Despite these limitations, opportunities to use my musical abilities have not diminished. I enjoy accompanying at the church and teaching twenty-one piano students.

No longer can I go skiing with the family, which had been one of my greatest pleasures. My left leg would not be able to respond quickly when needing to stop or turn. My knee will not bend completely either. While they are skiing, I use my time in other ways—like completing this book.

May you be uplifted and compelled to draw close to the One who made you, who loves you enough to send his Son Jesus to pay for your sins and accept His forgiveness and cleansing. You then will be His child and have victory for life.

Victory does not mean getting all the things you want and ask for. He chose this time to answer in the affirmative all the prayers that went up on my behalf. He was not obligated. He allows hard places to come into our lives to develop our faith and dependence on Him more precisely. Our focus must be kept on our Lord God—His purity, His holiness, His righteousness. We must seek to honor and obey His Word, the Holy Bible, desiring to glorify Him in all our words and deeds.

> *"The Lord your God is in your midst,*
> *A victorious warrior.*
> *He will exult over you with joy.*
> *He will be quiet in His love,*
> *He will rejoice over you with shouts of joy."*
>   Zephaniah 3:17

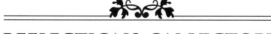

REFLECTIONS ON VICTORY

Our victorious Warrior loves us with steady, emotional excitement!

> *"The LORD your God is in your midst, a victorious warrior. He will exult over you with joy, He will be quiet in His love, He will rejoice over you with shouts of joy."*
>   Zephaniah 3:17

Are you experiencing victory?

Describe your warrior.

Quest for Love

Lord, Your love for me is hard to comprehend...
So unselfish in giving me eternal life,
So understanding of my heart's requests,
So tender towards my falling tears,
So willing to bear my heaviest loads,
So generous in supplying life's necessities,
And so humble — to be the King of Kings!
Lord, give me a love that penetrates the lives of others,
that Christ may be seen in me...